theatre & human rights

Theatre &

Series Editors: Jen Harvie and Dan Rebellato

Published

Colette Conroy: *Theatre & the Body*
Jill Dolan: *Theatre & Sexuality*
Helen Freshwater: *Theatre & Audience*
Jen Harvie: *Theatre & The City*
Nadine Holdsworth: *Theatre & Nation*
Erin Hurley: *Theatre & Feeling*
Joe Kelleher: *Theatre & Politics*
Ric Knowles: *Theatre & Interculturalism*
Helen Nicholson: *Theatre & Education*
Lionel Pilkington: *Theatre & Ireland*
Paul Rae: *Theatre & Human Rights*
Dan Rebellato: *Theatre & Globalization*
Nicholas Ridout: *Theatre & Ethics*

Forthcoming

Susan Bennet: *Theatre & Museums*
Dominic Johnson: *Theatre & the Visual*
Caoime McAvinchey: *Theatre & Prison*
Bruce McConachie: *Theatre & Mind*
Juliet Rufford: *Theatre & Architecture*
Rebecca Schneider: *Theatre & History*

Theatre& Series
Series Standing Order
ISBN 978–0–230–20327–3

You can receive future titles in this series as they are published by placing a standing order. Please contact your bookseller or, in case of difficulty, write to us at the address below with your name and address, the title of the series and the ISBN quoted above.

Customer Services Department, Macmillan Distribution Ltd
Houndmills, Basingstoke, Hampshire RG21 6XS, England

---

theatre & human rights

Paul Rae

palgrave
macmillan

First published 2009 by
PALGRAVE MACMILLAN

Palgrave Macmillan in the UK is an imprint of Macmillan
Publishers Limited, registered in England, company number
785998, of Houndmills, Basingstoke, Hampshire RG21 6XS.

Palgrave Macmillan in the US is a division of St Martin's Press LLC,
175 Fifth Avenue, New York, NY 10010.

Palgrave Macmillan is the global academic imprint of the above
companies and has companies and representatives throughout
the world.

Palgrave® and Macmillan® are registered trademarks in the United
States, the United Kingdom, Europe and other countries.

ISBN-13: 978-0-230-20524-6 paperback
ISBN-10: 0-230-20524-0 paperback

This book is printed on paper suitable for recycling and made
from fully managed and sustained forest sources. Logging,
pulping and manufacturing processes are expected to conform to
the environmental regulations of the country of origin.

A catalogue record for this book is available from the British
Library.

A catalog record for this book is available from the Library of
Congress.

Printed and bound in China

contents

CONTENTS

series editors' preface

The theatre is everywhere, from entertainment districts to the fringes, from the rituals of government to the ceremony of the courtroom, from the spectacle of the sporting arena to the theatres of war. Across these many forms stretches a theatrical continuum through which cultures both assert and question themselves.

Theatre has been around for thousands of years, and the ways we study it have changed decisively. It's no longer enough to limit our attention to the canon of Western dramatic literature. Theatre has taken its place within a broad spectrum of performance, connecting it with the wider forces of ritual and revolt that thread through so many spheres of human culture. In turn, this has helped make connections across disciplines; over the past fifty years, theatre and performance have been deployed as key metaphors and practices with which to rethink gender, economics, war, language, the fine arts, culture and one's sense of self.

Theatre & is a long series of short books which hopes to capture the restless interdisciplinary energy of theatre and performance. Each book explores connections between theatre and some aspect of the wider world, asking how the theatre might illuminate the world and how the world might illuminate the theatre. Each book is written by a leading theatre scholar and represents the cutting edge of critical thinking in the discipline.

We have been mindful, however, that the philosophical and theoretical complexity of much contemporary academic writing can act as a barrier to a wider readership. A key aim for these books is that they should all be readable in one sitting by anyone with a curiosity about the subject. The books are challenging, pugnacious, visionary sometimes and, above all, clear. We hope you enjoy them.

Jen Harvie and Dan Rebellato

foreword

Paul Rae gathers in his book a plethora of events and practices related to the matter of theatre and human rights; in so doing, he challenges the reader with some paradoxical, complex issues concerning the role of the theatre today. On a personal level, I found myself intrigued and moved by Rae's interrogations; I tried to find a doorway into his topic from the viewpoint of the theatre's relationship to the trial.

In countries that are either engaged in war or on the brink of a new war, the security state suddenly awakens and confronts the civil state. Its first violent act is to impose martial law and suspend conventional judgment, and by the same token the rights of the citizens. The latter have no choice but to consent; objection is not allowed and is considered suspicious because it threatens the nation and its security. In the presence of danger, there is no time for lawful discussions and speeches....

In view of this threat, when the civil state finds itself weakened in the presence of the security state, and the regular workings of the courts are cancelled, what is left of theatre?

Trials have always provided a fertile soil for the theatre, because of the theatrical elements they carry: from the attorney who represents the accused to the judge who represents justice, from the re-enacting of the crime and the reasons behind it to the narrating of the events, from the statements and interrogation of the accused to his confrontation with the witnesses, from the specially designed costumes to the hammer declaring the adjourning of the session....

By definition, the trial gathers two opposing parties to confront one another verbally in front of a judge, each of them exposing their own point of view, defending it through various speeches and statements, presenting evidence and alibis, in the presence of a public intent on listening and witnessing, and awaiting the final decision of the judge who officiates in the name of law and justice.

In theatre as in courts, the trial takes place in front of an audience, the only difference being that the theatre, at least in principle, does not issue any judgments in favour of this or that party. It satisfies itself with the exposition of the case at hand, from its different angles, leaving enough breathing space for the audience to build their own opinions and decisions. Theatre is the ideal medium to expose uneasy and complex matters and plunge into them. It is the place where questions are asked, without reaching conclusions or judgments. It is a place where ideas are formulated. Theatre is not a spokesperson for this or that side, regardless of its situation and even if it is a victim; because who or what is the victim is a point of contention, anyway.

Theatre is a quest for differences, and the raising of discussions between them. As for the simplification of complex matters by reducing them to the status of 'executioner and victim' and hiding behind the victim while pretending to defend him and fight for his rights, this is nothing but a cancellation of the 'other' by considering him an absolute enemy, and consequently cancelling the idea of the trial. In my opinion, this could be considered a terrorist act in itself. Theatre stresses differences rather than similarities; it stresses confrontation rather than agreement. It is a place for uncertainty, a place for the struggle of ideas; it is a space for open discussion concerning an unresolved issue, in the presence of an alert audience, which is listening to the different voices and the conflicts between the characters.

The theatre needs an audience composed of individual citizens, having the benefit of civic rights, the ability to choose and express their opinions, enough time to think and contemplate, and access to enough space to distance themselves from other individuals. These citizens operate within the parameters of the lawful state and its institutions, which are committed to organising the relationships between them, protecting their privileges and human rights, and preventing one single individual from rising to power.

Paul Rae's book suggests to us an intertwining, sinuous way of dealing with the subject of theatre and human rights. From his first sentence, he proposes to take us on an unaccommodated, challenging intellectual trip. His last sentence enables us to reach our destination, but without final judgment and without hammering the session to a close.

(Translated from the Arabic by Ziad Nawfal)

Born in Beirut in 1967, Rabih Mroué is an actor, director, playwright and Contributing Editor to TDR: The Drama Review. *His plays, performances and videos question definitions of theatre, the relationship between the space and form of performance and, consequently, how the performer relates to the audience. His works deal with issues that have been swept under the carpet in Lebanon's current political climate and draw much-needed attention to broader political and economic contexts by means of a semi-documentary theatre. His works include* The Inhabitants of Images *(2008) and* Looking for a Missing Employee *(2005).*

theatre & human rights

Introduction: against intuition

When casually expressed, opinions about the relationship between theatre and human rights tend to be at once impassioned and vague. Human rights are generally held to be worth fighting for, and theatre-making one way of fighting for them; theatre is thought to be a progressive activity, and addressing human rights themes one way of ensuring its social relevance. There is some truth to these sentiments, and in societies whose citizens enjoy a well-established human rights culture, they serve to make the link between staging human relationships and denouncing human rights violations seem intuitive, self-evident.

However, another reason for the haziness with which this relationship is articulated, as well as the strength of feeling it can arouse, is that it is more complex and contradictory than it first appears. From the thematic treatment of human rights issues in plays, to activist and participatory performances with explicit human rights agendas; from theatre-makers playing an advocacy role as public intellectuals and civil society actors, to performances that challenge human rights norms, to theatre itself coming under threat from human rights abuses; from theatre aesthetics echoing the formal legal and political contexts within which human rights law is enacted and challenged, to the theatricality queasily inherent in some of the most iconic and widely publicised human rights violations of recent years – all these phenomena colour the relationship between theatre and human rights today. As such, presuming an *inherent* sympathy between making theatre and safeguarding human rights does neither – and no one – any good. In this book, I consider many facets of this relationship and argue that, ultimately, each activity best serves the other by throwing its practices and underlying assumptions into relief. Intuitions, in short, are not always to be trusted.

In a moment, I start by surveying common understandings of the term 'human rights'. I go on in Part One, 'The Human Right to Theatre?', to outline the diverse ways theatre-makers have sought to promote human rights, as well as which rights are expressed through theatre practice itself. In Part Two, 'Thinking Theatre and Human Rights', I argue that the relationship between theatre and human rights might best be understood in terms of complementarity rather than in terms of one always being in the service of the other. The three extended examples I provide in Part Two lead me into Part Three, 'Theatres of Cruelty', about aspects of the theatre experience that are uncomfortably close to the dynamics of abuse. In my conclusion, I conduct one more exercise in 'thinking theatre and human rights', which raises questions about the future of the relationship and suggests a more nuanced way of understanding it than the one I glossed in my opening paragraph.

First, though, a few words on my approach to the topic. My rule of thumb in selecting examples has been to respect both the range of theatrical approaches and the scope of human rights, by being as open as possible to different styles of performance and to diverse geographical and cultural locations. 'As possible' underscores the parameters of any such project, and it will soon become apparent how this discussion reflects what I have been able to see, read, learn and think as a moderately well-travelled British national and long-term resident of the Southeast Asian city-state of Singapore.

It is important to stress, though, that parameters are not the same as limitations. Any reflexive enquiry into the theatre *or* human rights must contend at some point with the relationship between the specific and the general, and establishing parameters is one way of mediating between the two. Plays are written, workshops conducted and performances staged at specific times and in particular places; understanding this context keys us in to the details of the event, but it also provides the basis for comparison with other events, as well as grounds for more widely applicable assertions about what theatre is and does. Similarly, how 'human rights' are interpreted, practised or violated in individual situations has a bearing on claims for their universality.

Married by that apparently innocuous ampersand, 'Theatre & Human Rights' express the specific–general dynamic in numerous guises, which I account for where I can. I have combined discussions of particular perform-ances, well-known practices and classic plays; I have aimed to balance the immediate demand that suffering makes of us, and the urgency of the theatre produced in response, with the reflective and measured tone that characterises much human rights theory; and I have given space to some of the more 'radical' critiques of the liberal idea of human rights, while acknowledging the importance of consensus and moderation in getting things done on a global scale.

I consider these tensions a characteristic of the rela-tionship between theatre and human rights, rather than a problem to be solved. But don't take my word for it. There will always be more to say, especially about context, than a short, sharp book such as this can accommodate. The 'Further reading' section provides suggestions for fleshing out the discussions that follow and for opening new lines of enquiry.

One more parameter bears flagging up. With a few exceptions, I have restricted my focus in this book to the-atrical performances and practices. However, my approach owes a critical debt to the more expansive discipline of per-formance studies, as well as to important work in that field that lies beyond the scope of the present study. Although it has provided me with a means of thinking across theatri-cal forms and of understanding their place within a wider social context of performative actions and meaning-making processes, I do not have the space here to do justice to the work of scholars such as the late Dwight Conquergood. His politically committed analyses of social and judicial violence and highly reflexive work with culturally marginalised communities laid the ground for a mode of activist scholarship that is strongly informed by human rights concerns. For examples of this approach, see *The SAGE Handbook of Performance Studies* (2006), edited by D. Soyini Madison and Judith Hamera, and *Violence Performed* (2008), edited by Patrick Anderson and Jisha Menon.

Part One

the human right to theatre?

Rights talk

When the freedom to make or watch theatre is threatened, especially by states or institutions, human rights are often perceived to be at stake. But ask the people around you to name some human rights, and 'theatre' is unlikely to be one of them. Understanding this apparent paradox requires that we survey how theatre has been used to address the *subject* of human rights (for example, in being about freedom of expression) and outline the ways in which theatre is itself the *object* of those rights (for example, as an exercise in freedom of expression). First, though, it is useful to clarify what the term 'human rights' conventionally means.

A clue can be found in 'Art, Truth and Politics', a lecture given by the British playwright Harold Pinter on accepting the 2005 Nobel Prize in Literature. At a time of heightened geo-political tensions, the prize was widely taken to recognise Pinter's track record on human rights advocacy as much as the quality of his writing. Indeed, the Nobel committee signalled this in their appropriately terse announcement of the prize, which stated simply that Pinter 'uncovers the precipice under everyday prattle and forces entry into oppression's closed rooms'.

True to form, Pinter's lecture combined reflections on the writing process with a coruscating and contentious attack on the 'systematic, constant, vicious, remorseless' crimes perpetrated by the United States through its foreign policy since the end of the Second World War. As we shall see, although Pinter did not use the term 'human rights' specifically, the time-frame of his analysis was significant, as was the way he chose to conclude. Having described as 'mandatory' the obligation all of us have to define the truth of our lives and our societies, he warned: 'If such a determination is not embodied in our political vision we have no hope of restoring what is so nearly lost to us – the dignity of man.'

The reference to 'dignity' was pointed, for the term has historically underpinned the moral appeal to a set of human values existing independently of the laws and customs of particular states or societies. Any rights that can be shown to follow from these values (rather, say, than those rights owed a citizen by dint of nationality) can therefore be described as human rights. In the Western tradition, one of the earliest extant and oft-cited explorations of this idea is Sophocles' Theban tragedy *Antigone* (*c*.441 BCE), whose titular heroine flouts the laws of the city-state to observe burial rites for her slain brother, the traitor Polynices. Fearing any threat to the recently becalmed 'ship of state' (l. 189) (as well as to his own self-interest), Antigone's uncle, King Creon, sentences her to be buried alive. Refusing to suborn her dignity to 'such crude laws' (l. 938), Antigone somewhat impetuously embraces her fate in the name of blood ties and of 'the great unwritten, unshakable traditions' (l. 505), traditions embodying an apparently timeless justice impervious to the worldly concerns of mortals.

Two millennia later, the Enlightenment saw a revival of interest in this idea of a pre-social moral or spiritual law, which would inform much Euro-American thinking about rights. This thinking included John Locke's (1632–1704) concept of natural rights (to life, liberty and property), Immanuel Kant's (1724–1804) right to freedom (leading to civil, international and cosmopolitan rights), and proclamations and treatises such as the French Declaration of the Rights of Man and the Citizen (1789), the American Bill of Rights (1791), Thomas Paine's *Rights of Man* (1791–2) and Mary Wollstonecraft's *A Vindication of the Rights of Woman* (1792).

Although the influence of these ideas would be long-lasting, they would not go unchallenged. It is perhaps testament to the richness of Sophocles' play that *Antigone* would subsequently be invoked by the German philosopher G. W. F. Hegel (1770–1831) in his *critique* of natural law, particularly as it related to Kant's assumption that human subjects were rational and autonomous. For Hegel, neither Creon nor Antigone is entirely in the right. Rather, their tragedy lies in failing to recognise how much their apparently opposed and principled positions are in fact interdependent products of their particular situation.

As presented in his *Phenomenology of Spirit* (1807), Hegel's argument is dense and complex. But the basic point about rights and values being embedded in – and contingent on – human communities and social relations (and not naturally determined) is one that has exercised philosophers and rights theorists from a range of political perspectives. Early examples, collected by Jeremy Waldron in *Nonsense upon Stilts* (1987), include the utilitarian Jeremy Bentham (1748–1832), who dismissed idealistic talk of rights as just that, 'nonsense upon stilts', arguing instead that they were a product of rational self-interest. Karl Marx (1818–83), meanwhile, felt that documents such as the French Declaration privileged the bourgeois individual and downplayed the social and economic conditions that impeded the flourishing of 'men', rather than 'man'.

As a widespread and long-standing cultural form whose expressions are always time- and place-specific, it is little surprise that the theatre has continued to keep pace with such debates. It is telling, for instance, that *Antigone* has itself seen numerous re-workings in response to changing times and circumstances, not least those by Jean Anouilh (Théâtre de l'Atelier, 1944) and Bertolt Brecht (1948), which were reactions to one of the most cataclysmic events of the twentieth century, the Second World War. Indeed, the year that the Berliner Ensemble premiered Brecht's rather wishful version at the Stadttheater Chur in neutral Switzerland also saw the proclamation of the most significant human rights document of the modern period, the Universal Declaration of Human Rights. Drafted in the aftermath of the war by a committee that included representatives from America, Europe, Lebanon and China, the Declaration sought to strengthen the rights provisions laid out in the United Nations Charter (1945). Although it drew substantially on aspects of Enlightenment thinking, the Declaration was the first such document to affirm the indivisibility, inalienability and inviolability of certain rights for *all* human beings, and it is here we find the language alluded to by Pinter in his Nobel lecture. Adopted by the UN General Assembly on 10 December 1948, the Declaration begins by stating that 'recognition of the inherent dignity and of the equal and inalienable rights of all members of the human family is the foundation of freedom, justice and peace in the world'. Article 1 goes on: 'All human beings are born free and equal in dignity and rights. They are endowed with reason and conscience and should act towards one another in a spirit of brotherhood.' From that develop twenty-nine further articles, dealing with, among other things, security and protection (from discrimination, violence and persecution), freedom (of thought, belief, assembly, expression and movement), participation (in political, cultural and family life) and fair treatment before the law.

Today, more than sixty years on, the world has changed substantially, and the field of human rights is vastly more complex. In 1966, International Covenants on Civil and Political Rights and on Economic, Social and Cultural Rights were introduced to specify aspects of the Declaration in more detail and to make their protection legally binding. These covenants were followed by further agreements, known as 'instruments', that addressed specific areas of concern, including racial discrimination (1966), discrimination against women (1979), torture (1984) and the rights of the child (1989). Regional human rights charters have been ratified in Europe (1950), the Americas (1969) and Africa (1981) and by the League of Arab States (2004). In 2006 the United Nations replaced its Commission on Human Rights with a beefed-up Human Rights Council, and in 2007 the Association of Southeast Asian Nations (ASEAN) took an initial step towards redressing a notable lack of human rights provisions in the region by announcing the inclusion of an appropriate mechanism in its new charter.

These legal initiatives have been accompanied by the growth of a panoply of national and international public and non-governmental organisations (NGOs) which promote respect for human rights, campaign against their abuse and monitor the implementation of relevant legislation. Meanwhile, academics, activists, policy-makers and politicians debate terminologies, concepts and arguments in a sometimes highly specialised human rights discourse. Their concerns range from identifying the underlying principles of human rights, to the politics of rights-based legislation and action, to the practicalities of policing human rights abuses.

Perhaps one of the most significant testaments to the influence of the Declaration and to human rights as a way of thinking about the world and our place in it lies in the prevalence of 'rights talk' among those with little or no knowledge of these official frameworks. Available in more than 360 languages, the Declaration is the world's most widely translated document. For a first-time reader in English, there will be a familiar ring to many terms and phrases – 'Everyone has the right to life, liberty and security of person' (Article 3), 'No one shall be subjected to torture or to cruel, inhuman or degrading treatment or punishment' (Article 5). Indeed, the discussion of human rights – what they are, whether they are respected or abused, what responsibilities they entail, their proper place and weight within domestic legislation – is integral to the public life of many societies, and its terminology permeates the conversations and perceptions of many citizens.

Theatre and the subject of human rights

As professional attention-grabbers, it is unsurprising that theatre-makers have a long history of outspokenness in just such conversations, particularly where they believe voices have been inappropriately silenced or perspectives ignored. However, the relationship between theatre and human rights seldom runs smooth, and with power comes vulnerability. For every Arthur Miller, David Hare and Tom Stoppard (campaigners for freedom of expression with writer's organisations such as International PEN and Index on Censorship) or Lillian Hellman (whose estate funds the Hellman/Hammett grants, awarded annually by Human Rights Watch to writers in financial need as a result of expressing their views), there are theatre-makers who have themselves endured exile, detention or worse for their political and/or artistic positions. These include Brazil's Augusto Boal, Chile's Ariel Dorfman, the Czech Republic's Václav Havel, Nigeria's Wole Soyinka, Kenya's Ngugi Wa Thiong'o, India's Safdar Hashmi, Singapore's Kuo Pao Kun and Indonesia's W. S. Rendra.

The actions and experiences of these individuals point to an easily overlooked aspect of how the theatre has itself been used to address the subject of human rights: it tends to focus less on human rights per se than on their abuse. In part, this underscores the progressive role of theatre-makers in wider traditions of civil activism. But it also suggests that there is something rather untheatrical about the nature of human rights: simply stated, one does not *do* them in the same way as one *violates* them. As James Nickel puts it in *Making Sense of Human Rights* (2007, pp. 61–5) the main concerns of such rights are the securities and freedoms that make it possible both to *have* and to *lead* a life. To the extent they are respected, they recede from discourse or dispute into enactment and experience. Enshrined in domestic legislation and tacitly observed in day-to-day interactions among individuals and in their treatment by the authorities, such rights inhere in the fabric of society.

The theme of human rights

In contrast, human rights abuses often take the form of discrete acts that stand out from social norms. As Todd Landman notes in *Studying Human Rights* (2006), a common strategy employed by truth commissions to catalogue abuses is the 'who did what to whom' model (p. 110). For social scientists, this model provides a means of quantifying otherwise disparate events and contested experiences by zeroing in on the core components of the violation. But the phrase 'who did what to whom' also has strong dramaturgical connotations, and in this formal correspondence we find a starting-point for surveying the diverse ways in which theatre is used to address human rights themes.

As theatre-making entails the ordering of meanings and materials in time and space, staging 'who did what to whom' is a process of structuring and representing events and their contexts. The styles and techniques employed for this purpose will also influence how these events are interpreted, first by the theatre-makers themselves, and subsequently by audiences. On both counts, such interpretations may range from the fractured to the didactic, but they will assuredly be there. Even in documentary formats (such as so-called verbatim theatre, discussed below in the 'Paralegal performance' section), source materials are often edited and performed so as to respect theatrical conventions of narrative. For example, *My Name Is Rachel Corrie* (Royal Court, 2005), excerpted from the journals of an American peace activist killed by an Israeli Defence Force bulldozer, and co-edited by Katherine Viner and Alan Rickman, is notable for the poignancy of its character development.

Performances that focus on the representation of 'who did what to whom' serve to grant the event a local habitation and a name: specific abuses are depicted within a designated context. Often performed primarily for the community in which they originate (which can lead critics to underestimate the prevalence of the approach), many such productions retain this sense of localised address even when they travel. Take, for instance, the several dozen contenders for Amnesty International's annual Freedom of Expression Award, which recognises the play at the Edinburgh Fringe Festival that best contributes to 'the public's greater awareness and understanding of human rights issues'. Diverse in form and origin, the artists often have a historical or geographical connection with their topic, and a key aim in performing at the festival is consciousness-raising. At other times, artists amplify the scope of their concerns at home and the urgency of their message abroad by refracting them through more internationally recognisable material. Such was the case with the Belarus Free Theatre's *Being Harold Pinter* (2007), which spliced together Pinter's Nobel lecture and excerpts from some of his plays with accounts of political oppression in Belarus and was performed in Europe and Australia.

Being Harold Pinter depicts a political situation where the oppressive power relations are reasonably clear-cut. However, individual human rights violations are often extremely complex events, and for a variety of social and psychological reasons those caught up in them may have difficulty understanding what took place. Here, structure may be just as significant as representation. In workshops and projects involving active participation, theatrical representations of the *what* of human rights abuses can also foster an exploration of the *how* and the *why*. The range of rights issues that can be addressed in this way is vast, but among the most challenging situations are conflict and post-conflict zones. For instance, In Place of War, a Manchester University-based research project, documents social theatre initiatives in Rwanda, Sri Lanka, Northern Ireland and Palestine/Israel, and with UK-based refugees (www.inplaceofwar.net). Diverse in terms of local context, many such projects use theatre as a structured means of investigating competing interpretations of the past, and so addressing the legacies and continuing effects of conflict.

In the process of separating out, debating and staging 'who', 'what' and 'whom', then, theatre can draw attention to otherwise overlooked human rights abuses and contribute to processes of understanding and reconciliation. Such productions often take the form of grassroots initiatives that address unique situations, though they may expand their terms of reference in order to tour.

Other projects generalise even more widely by addressing common, rather than particular, experiences of abuse. An example is the testimonial genre, which includes Ariel Dorfman's *Speak Truth to Power: Voices from Beyond the Dark* (Kennedy Centre for the Performing Arts, Washington DC, 2000), about human rights defenders, and *The Exonerated* (Actor's Gang, Los Angeles, 2002) by Jessica Blank and Eric Jensen, based on the testimonies of American death-row inmates whose convictions had been overturned. The best known, however, is Eve Ensler's *The Vagina Monologues* (HERE Arts Center, New York, 1996). Her self-consciously empowering monologues about female sexual and reproductive experiences have been translated into more than twenty languages and are performed annually in hundreds of venues globally to mark the V-Day campaign to stop violence against women.

One noteworthy feature of this genre is the generation of source material through interviews that are often then edited and conflated. This channelling of diverse and multiple voices no doubt contributes to the plays' popular appeal, as well as to their amplification across media, through extensive coverage, celebrity involvement, and film and print spin-offs. Although 'who did what to whom' remains a motivating factor, such work tends to reveal patterns of abuse across contexts, and its address is accordingly general rather than local.

The 'human' in human rights

In broad terms, this discussion suggests that one way of distinguishing among different theatrical approaches to the subject of human rights lies in how they inflect the meaning of the term 'subject'. When the primary focus is 'who did what to whom', 'subject' is best understood as 'theme'. Meanwhile, performances that speak both for and to a wider public underscore the word's philosophical connotations, as in 'subjectivity', and remind us that, whatever else it is, the subject of human rights is also the human being.

Even here differences in approach can be discerned. It is noticeable, for instance, that the testimonial form tends to privilege the personalised voice. Even where the text is composite and the narrator unnamed, it speaks of and to the individual, whose self-actualisation remains the most important step towards redressing the wrongs depicted. A contrasting approach is exemplified by the activist strategies of the Theatre of the Oppressed, which was first developed by Augusto Boal in the 1970s. Today, the International Theatre of the Oppressed Organisation, whose objective is 'the development of essential Human Rights' (www.theatreoftheoppressed.org), boasts affiliates all over the world. Its practitioners use a range of participatory techniques, including 'forum theatre' – where 'spect-actors' intervene in the staging of a contentious everyday scenario – to enable disadvantaged people to understand the structural reasons for their oppression and to empower them to change their situation.

In its focus on systems, rather than discrete instances, of abuse, the Theatre of the Oppressed might be seen as a grassroots corollary to the testimonial genre. In some ways, this is an unlikely pairing. Politically, the latter conforms to a liberal model of the self-contained subject in privileging the monologic mode. The Theatre of the Oppressed takes a more radical approach, where humans are seen as inherently social beings whose potential is best realised through dialogue and collective action. Taken together, however, they hint at the range of human rights-related theatre whose impetus is basically humanist: as the subject of human rights, either the human is the free agent of his or her own realisation or in that realisation the human becomes free.

Human rights in society

Nevertheless, the later development of Boal's work points towards a more complex scenario. In contrast to his early focus on the socially and economically marginalised classes, his therapeutic techniques, known as 'the Rainbow of Desire', address the psychological effects of living in a capitalist society, and he developed his so-called Legislative Theatre upon his election to political office in the early 1990s. Boal's trajectory suggests that neither self-understanding nor social analysis may be as straightforward as he first described them in *Theatre of the Oppressed* (1979), which raises yet another meaning of the term 'subject'. The subject *of* human rights may be the human, but the human is subject *to* psychological desires and political forces that act upon him or her in unforeseen ways.

Rights-themed theatre that seeks to capture this complexity is not easily subsumed into a conventional format. Groupov's *Rwanda 94* (Gymnase Aubanel, Avignon, 1999), a Rwandan–Belgian collaboration about the 1994 genocide, lasted six hours and combined documentary footage, eyewitness testimony, historical reconstruction, original songs and music, facts, figures and fictional scenes. Subtitled 'An Attempt at Symbolic Repatriation to the Dead, for Use by the Living', it is a reminder that no single story can communicate the immensity or the horror of what took place, and no one representation can explain or resolve it. However, in drawing together a variety of presentational modes and interpretive strategies, the piece underscores the multiplicity of contributing factors that make up both a traumatic event and its afterlives, including psychological drives, individual actions, institutional politics, media representations, cultural memories and historical forces.

Such is the complexity of 'the subject of human rights' that it is arguably better served by a theatre that reflects that complexity than by one that seeks to resolve it. However, where some performances, such as *Rwanda 94*, reflect the radical instability of meanings and motivations during times of crisis, other theatre-makers have proved adept at distilling such complexities, thereby making them widely resonant. It is striking, for instance, that rights-related concerns inform some of the most widely staged and studied plays of the post-war period. The continuing international appeal of many such plays to performers and audiences alike signals qualities that substantially exceed the initial contexts of their presentation. Such works may explore questions that are of particular relevance to the theatre, such as language (Václav Havel's *The Memorandum* [1965], Brian Friel's *Translations* [1980], Harold Pinter's *Mountain Language* [1988]), psychology (Ariel Dorfman's *Death and the Maiden* [1990]), spectacle (Suzan Lori-Parks' *Venus* [1996], Caryl Churchill's *Far Away* [2000]) or the relationship between the public and the private (Liz Lochhead's *Mary Queen of Scots Got Her Head Chopped Off* [1987], Caryl Churchill's *Mad Forest* [1990]). Or they may provide fresh insights into familiar themes, such as state violence (Dario Fo's *Accidental Death of an Anarchist* [1970]), political oppression (Athol Fugard's *Antigone*-inspired *The Island* [1973]), genocide (Peter Weiss' *The Investigation* [1965]), competing value systems (Wole Soyinka's *Death and the King's Horseman* [1975]) and discrimination (Ama Ata Aidoo's *Anowa* [1970], Martin Sherman's *Bent* [1979]).

But these thematic attributions are oversimplifications. Here, 'who did what to whom' is at once central and incidental; 'human rights' is as much a means to an end as an end in itself. Plays such as these gather up the various meanings of the term 'subject' that have been explored above and remind us that 'the subject of human rights' is both a distinct topic and an aspect of thought and action that suffuses all areas of social existence. They explore the point at which rights concerns inhere into the fabric of a society, and their continuing appeal signals the extent to which they themselves constitute a unique strand of that fabric.

In a different way, the same might be said of certain long-term community theatre projects. Activist interventions are by nature short and sharp – in *Theatre of the Oppressed*, Boal describes his techniques as a 'rehearsal for revolution' (p. 141) – but the moment of advocacy cannot be sustained indefinitely. The reality of rights work, as well as the practicalities of theatrical collaboration, means an incremental approach can also bear fruit. In his 'tactical notebook' *Action Theatre: Initiating Changes* (2007), the Bangladeshi theatre activist Motahar Akand outlines an eight-step process, beginning with a fifteen- to ninety-day period of rapport-building, during which the foundations are laid for a participatory theatre project within a given community. This is followed by research into local conditions and the development, dramatisation, rehearsal and performance of a story that demonstrates a specific instance of abuse. The ensemble then encourages the community to act, in the first instance by identifying an appropriate resolution to the scenario depicted, and subsequently by taking follow-up action to guard against its recurrence. Importantly, the final step is 'institutionalisation', where the group establishes a long-term base and integrates its work into the warp and weft of the community, so that 'it becomes sustainable like a school or a library' (p. 11).

It is an intriguing model, and one that may hold lessons for practitioners and audiences of many kinds. Community and other kinds of 'social' theatre, multimedia performances, documentary dramas, festival productions and well-made plays all provide a means of holding our actions, our selves and our societies up to scrutiny in light of human rights concerns. Individual productions can do this with great force, but 'who did what to whom' is never an isolated incident – and neither is the theatre that reports it. In many cultures the theatre is, itself, an institution, and understanding the implications of this for its relationship with human rights requires that we approach it from a different angle.

Theatre as an object of human rights

As an inherently social activity, the theatre provides a distinctive platform for addressing human rights issues, and theatre-makers have demonstrated a tradition of active participation in related debates both within and beyond the confines of the stage. As an art form operating at the charged point where lives are given voice and experiences form, and where representatives of one group can make their address to others, the theatre is well placed to bring to light behaviour that contests or contravenes human rights standards.

These observations provide a baseline understanding of theatre's place in the field of human rights. Yet identifying a production's significance solely in its treatment of human rights issues is invariably reductive and may obscure other aspects of its argument and realisation. For example, Dorfman's *Death and the Maiden* is ostensibly about a traumatised torture victim, Paulina Salas, and her desire for retribution when a man she believes to have been one of her torturers, Roberto Miranda, chances to drop off her husband, Gerardo, after his car gets a puncture. But the *interest* of the play — indeed, its thrilling and vertiginous emotional force — lies first and foremost in how this scenario inflects ordinary human relationships, both between intimates and between strangers. Uncertainty over Roberto's true identity, and Paulina's and Gerardo's conflicting positions on revenge and forgiveness, corrode the foundations on which audience members can have faith in even the most banal of the characters' pronouncements. The key to the play lies not in the apparently climactic confessions of violent wrongdoing but in such small moments of compromised and achingly commonplace truth as when Paulina, speaking of Gerardo, admits to Roberto that 'we lied to each other out of love' (p. 140).

So although *Death and the Maiden* is often framed — not least by Dorfman himself — as a human rights play, I would argue that an important part of its appeal lies in the *ambiguity* of its position on human rights. It reminds us how difficult it can be to maintain the indivisibility and inalienability of such rights — central tenets of the Universal Declaration — under all circumstances. It may even suggest the impossibility of doing so under certain conditions: an impossibility that says more about the vicissitudes of the human condition than it does about the moral strictures of human rights.

Thus, although theatre can be set to work in the service of any number of human rights, and although certain qualities of the art form may encourage theatre-makers to do such work, these cannot be the reasons people cry foul on human rights grounds when theatre is threatened. After all, a given performance need not have a human rights theme to merit defending; it may even call accepted truths about certain rights into question. Rather, such a reaction is elicited because the freedom to make and watch theatre is the *object* of numerous basic rights. Exactly which depends on the instruments one is referring to and on how well one believes they apply to the theatre. Some, such as Article 27(2) of the Universal Declaration, 'Everyone has the right to the protection of the moral and material interests resulting from any scientific, literary or artistic production of which he is the author,' relate rather ambiguously, given the collective nature of theatre-making. In what follows, I discuss the three rights in the Declaration that I believe are most pertinent.

Article 19. Everyone has the right to freedom of opinion and expression

With its roots in the European Enlightenment, this is sometimes described as a 'first-generation' right. In part as a result of this historically and culturally specific heritage, it is also one of the most contentious. During the 1990s, for instance, some East Asian governments characterised freedom of expression as exemplifying a 'Western' attitude that privileged the rights of the individual to the detriment of society as a whole. In turn, those governments were criticised for suppressing rights as a means of privileging their own interests over democratic participation and accountability.

Given how often freedom-of-expression debates rage over questions of truth, the theatre's notorious unreliability on such matters only complicates its relationship to the right. For instance, when an anal rape scene in Howard Brenton's *The Romans in Britain* (National Theatre, London, 1980) resulted in the British director Michael Bogdanov being tried for 'procuring an act of gross indecency between men', it was on the grounds that there was no difference between the act and its representation. The judge agreed. At other times, the artifice of the theatrical enterprise can ensure – like King Lear's long-suffering indulgence of his 'all-licensed fool' – greater critical or interpretive latitude than is tolerated in society as a whole. Powerful figures have long been lampooned or satirised theatrically in ways that, in other media, could result in a defamation suit or worse.

This ambiguity over *what* is being expressed by theatre-makers is exacerbated by the fact that, whereas freedom of *thought* is commonly held to be an absolute right, there is less agreement on whether the resulting thoughts should be articulated at all costs, particularly where other rights risk being infringed. In the theatre, this question most often arises in cases of censorship, where the work may be judged to threaten national security (in the case of inflammatory material), offend public decency (in the case of obscenity) or abuse the rights of specific groups (in the case of blasphemy or so-called hate speech). In Britain in 2004, these issues crystallised around Gurpreet Kaur Bhatti's play *Bezhti*, whose run at the Birmingham Repertory Theatre was cut short when protests from some local Sikhs, objecting to depictions of rape and murder in a *gurdwara* (temple), spilled over into violence.

Although in the case of *Bezhti* it was the producing theatre that decided to withdraw the play amid concerns for audience safety, more generally, legal 'best practice' dictates that there be clear 'limitations on limitations', so that any resulting restrictions imposed by the authorities are transparent and proportionate. The fundamental arbitrariness of censorship means that this is often not the case – but also that systems of regulation can be vulnerable. In Britain, a series of disputes precipitated by Edward Bond's play *Saved* (Royal Court, 1965) led to the outright collapse of the theatre censorship regime in 1968. Elsewhere, necessarily anecdotal evidence from theatre-makers of my acquaintance suggests that censors can be more open to negotiation and incremental change than they officially acknowledge, although the public expression of rights-based grievances on the part of artists can lead to the hardening of positions by the authorities.

Other kinds of restriction on freedom of expression may be harder to address, because they are less direct than the outright censorship of specific material. They may take the form, for instance, of the open or covert withholding of permits or funding. This was initially the case with the so-called NEA 4 – four American performance artists who were refused National Endowment of the Arts funding in 1989 because of the sexually challenging nature of their work. The artists appealed successfully, only for subsequent work to encounter difficulties because of an alleged lack of artistic merit, a criterion explicitly linked in a 1990 law (upheld by the Supreme Court in 1998) to a 'decency test'. Patrician institutions have long styled themselves the arbiters of both taste and decency, and as creative and cultural production falls increasingly within the remit of the globalised 'knowledge economy', the censor-critic – who claims to judge on relative merit, rather than absolute standards of morality – is set to become one of the most intractable obstacles to freedom of expression in the theatre, and one of the most difficult to challenge.

Article 20(1): Everyone has the right to freedom of peaceful assembly and association

Today, few theatre-goers in societies where rights are broadly respected would consciously claim to be exercising their right to free assembly. Nevertheless, the history of the theatre in many parts of the world is closely aligned with that of civic participation. In a globalising world where human communication is increasingly mediated at a distance, this basic fact of co-presence (to say nothing of collective processes of imagining and interpretation) continues to grant theatre much of its force – and, in the eyes of certain regimes, its threat. The Free Theatre of Belarus reports staging clandestinely advertised performances in private houses and apartments, and being raided by armed police;

China's now-thriving performance art scene began as an underground network of private events.

Even in authoritarian regimes that are less heavy-handed, the sociality of the theatre event renders it susceptible to regulation, requiring what is effectively a calibrated exemption from stringent restrictions on public assembly. In Singapore, for example, most plays require an Arts Entertainment Licence. The licence application is assessed by a government body upon submission of a script and details about the venue and performers. The licence advises, among other things, that performers refrain from mingling with the audience and that, if they do, it be for not more than fifteen minutes. Indeed, for a decade from the early 1990s, forum theatre and performance art were proscribed on the grounds that unscripted performances risked public disorder.

This, in turn, reminds us that, alongside freedom of assembly, theatre can also be an object of the rights to free association and to protest – rights strikingly exercised, for example, by politicised theatre-makers in parts of East Asia (such as Taiwan, Indonesia and the Philippines) and South America (notably Mexico, Argentina and Brazil).

Article 27(1): Everyone has the right freely to participate in the cultural life of the community, to enjoy the arts and to share in scientific advancement and its benefits

The Universal Declaration made only minimal reference to cultural rights in 1948, but globalisation has made the need to safeguard the languages and cultural practices of minorities, in particular, increasingly pressing. The rights subsequently articulated in documents such as the Declaration on the Rights of Persons Belonging to National or Ethnic, Religious or Linguistic Minorities (1992) are sometimes described as 'third-generation' rights, because they post-date the Declaration and go beyond its 'second-generation' focus on social, economic and cultural rights to encompass environmental factors and collective rights. They are contentious for some theorists because, by definition, they cannot be applied equally to everyone, which calls their universality into question. On the other hand, one may argue that human cultural and genetic diversity is a good in and of itself, that it benefits all humankind, simply by demonstrating as comprehensively as possible what it means to be human.

To be sure, there is the possibility of cultural ghettoisation. Although legislating for such rights aims at the integration of minorities into the social and economic mainstream, promoting their arts and theatre may risk turning out museum pieces, weighed down by the dead hand of 'tradition'. But this would be to underestimate performance's relative importance to many such minorities, for whom it serves not only as a vital means of transmitting the language, beliefs and cultural memories of the group but as a significant point of interface with the majority and others.

An interesting example of the complexities of this dynamic arose in Indonesia in 2006, when a coalition of Islamic political parties proposed an 'Anti-Pornography and Pornoaction Bill'. Along with representations of sexual activity, the Bill would have criminalised *pornoaksi* ('pornoaction') – a wide sweep of expressive and creative activities, from kissing in public to dressing and dancing 'immodestly'. The Bill was decried by artists and feminists (notably the playwright Ratna Sarumpaet) in many parts of Indonesia and met with particular consternation on the predominantly Hindu island of Bali. The Balinese objection was twofold: that the Bill would severely damage the tourist industry by restricting what tourists could wear and do (some locals described it as 'a third Bali bomb') and that, by proscribing numerous local dance and performance forms, it would compromise the Balinese way of life and sense of identity. It might be added that, given the centrality of performance to Bali's international reputation as a tourist hotspot, these objections were related.

In 2008, a revised draft was passed. However, opponents claim that requiring exempted performances to take place in designated spaces is too restrictive and that the definition of *pornoaksi* remains too open to interpretation, granting conservative activists licence to take remedial action where they believe the law to have been flouted. As for Bali, these uncertainties risk discouraging innovation and adaptation, thereby compromising its responsiveness to changing times and reducing its performing arts to the abovementioned status of museum pieces.

Performance ('theatre' may be too limiting or culturally specific a word here) is also central to the cultural rights of indigenous peoples, who number roughly 300 million worldwide. Against a common historical backdrop of cultural, economic and territorial marginalisation at the hands of settler communities, self-determination is a central tenet of indigenous rights. It is expressed through protection from cultural genocide and the right to practise, develop and transmit cultural traditions and customs. Self-determination extends to the right for a given group to self-identify *as* indigenous – and where written records do not exist, performance can play a defining role in a group's *sui generis* claim to being a rights-bearing entity.

A good example of how indigenous people have combined performance traditions and contemporary theatre to affirm their cultural rights is *Ngapartji Ngapartji* (2005 onwards), a community arts, performance and web-based project initiated by the Australian group Big hART. The title means 'I give you something, you give me something' in the aboriginal Pitjantjatjara language, and the community component of the project involves skills training in film, art and theatre-making. For outsiders, the project is centred on a series of language lessons which communicate different aspects of Pitjantjatjara culture and history. Online subscribers can take a course of multimedia lessons, created and performed by Pitjantjatjara community members in the area around Mparntwe/Alice Springs. The experience reproduces something of the processes of oral transmission by which such languages have traditionally been learnt. An accompanying theatre show combines language learning with the story of actor Trevor Jamieson's family during the Cold War. At that time, many members of his community were displaced from their lands in the Great Victoria Desert by nuclear testing, and others who were left behind as a result of political incompetence suffered radiation sickness.

It is indicative of the complex dynamics of third-generation rights, however, that although the term *Ngapartji Ngapartji* suggests a spirit of reciprocity, the political context of Jamieson's story signals the historical imbalances in what has been given and what taken away. The relatively recent granting of so-called Native Title to the land cannot easily compensate for the upheavals of the Pitjantjatjara people or for the poisoning of their sacred sites.

Nor are theatre-makers themselves beyond reproach. Article 31 of the United Nations Declaration on the Rights of Indigenous Peoples (2007) specifies the right to maintain, control, protect and develop cultural heritage, traditional knowledge and traditional cultural expressions, as well as any related intellectual property. Meanwhile, Article 46 of UNESCO's Principles and Guidelines for the Protection of the Heritage of Indigenous Peoples (1998) goes so far as to stipulate that '[a]rtists, writers and performers should refrain from incorporating elements derived from indigenous heritage into their works without the informed consent of the traditional owners'. The relevance of this for theatre-makers is borne out by writers such as Rustom Bharucha, whose *Theatre and the World* (1993) and *The Politics of Cultural Practice* (2000) are strongly critical of cultural appropriation, particularly of Asian forms by Euro-American practitioners for 'intercultural' performances.

Although theatre may be used to promote rights, therefore, and participation can be viewed as exercising freedom of expression and assembly and as affirming cultural self-determination, we should acknowledge that this is of varying significance, depending on the context. Often, these rights pull into focus *as* rights only when they are threatened or withheld, and even where theatre-making can be seen as enacting or claiming a right, there is nothing inherently virtuous in it. Despite their in-principle indivisibility, the expression of some rights needs to be carefully balanced against the protections afforded by others, and such calculations do not always sit well alongside the exacting commitments a successful performance can require of artists and audiences alike. A fuller understanding of the relationship between theatre and human rights requires that we take a view that is at once more careful and more critical.

Part Two

thinking theatre and human rights

...all too human

In Part Two, I argue that in addition to thinking *about* theatre *in relation to* human rights, we need to think theatre and human rights *together*, in a *complementary relation*. One reason for this is that theatre is a messy business at the best of times. In contrast to the kind of moral and legal clarity for which many human rights advocates strive, the majority of performances that relate to rights issues or practices do so in ways that are hard to disentangle from more worldly concerns and pursuits. If, as I have suggested, this is the case even in self-styled 'human rights plays' such as *Death and the Maiden*, it is all the more acute among the many productions where rights are at stake, even if not at issue.

A usefully (if paradoxically) schematic example of this is British playwright Martin Crimp's *Attempts on Her Life* (1997). Seventeen discrete but interrelated scenes construct a fragmented portrait of Anna/Anny/Anya/Anuschka, who is more a peripatetic 'an(n)yone' of the globalised age than a conventional character. In numerous scenes, unnamed narrators describe acts of violence and subjugation – ethnocide, terrorism, racism, sexual exploitation – in which 'she' variously figures as perpetrator and victim. However, such is the sprawling world of the play – Crimp stipulates that the play is 'for a company of actors whose composition should reflect the composition of the world beyond the theatre' (p. 202) – that the violence becomes woven into an intricate tapestry of urbanity, domesticity, nostalgia and commercialism. This does nothing to diminish its visceral force on stage, but it certainly complicates any identification of cause, effect or individual agency. As the double meaning of the title suggests, 'who did what to whom' is both a core concern of the play and impossible to establish with any certainty.

The play's exploration of rights-related themes is further nuanced by a range of presentational styles characteristic of postmodern media culture: some scenes appropriate the rhetoric of advertising or television news, others take the form of a sophisticated dinner party game or a movie pitch, and a few mimic the style of other playwrights. Strains of Pinter's *Mountain Language* can be heard in the scene 'Strangely!', where a woman is interrogated at a checkpoint by soldiers; 'Faith in Ourselves', which imagines an attack on a tradition-bound rural community, recalls the morally murky neo-Balkans of Howard Barker's similarly episodic *The Possibilities* (1987). In fact, lines such as 'The burning people running blazing between the fruit trees which bear their names, scorching the leaves, writhing on the blades of grass, while the soldiers stand by laughing' (p. 217) could be interpreted as a pastiche of a Barker scenario. But the scene achieves more than a knowing wink. The narrators build it towards a kind of cathartic appropriation of Anya's suffering for their own benefit:

> — …because Anya's valley is *our* valley. Anya's trees are *our* trees. Anya's family is the family to which we all belong.
> — So it's a universal thing. / *Obviously*
> — It's a universal thing in which we recognise, we strangely recognise ourselves. Our own world. Our own pain.
> — A universal thing which strangely … what? What? What?
> — Which strangely restores
> — Which strangely restores — I think it does — yes
> — our faith in ourselves. (pp. 219–20)

Speakers and audience alike are implicated in an act of rhetorical violence that echoes the actual destruction and desecration described earlier in the scene; Crimp thus demonstrates how the language of human rights can be used for self-serving ends. In the name of universal values, it smoothes the passage between recognising the plight of another and identifying it as one's own, cannibalising and diminishing the original suffering in the process.

The warning against talking up localised atrocities for 'our' universal instruction must be as keenly felt by theatre-makers as by anyone. The generalising impetus in any staging of suffering entails an ethical responsibility to those individuals, communities or cultures being represented. But if we should rightly be wary of naively expanding particular circumstances to serve the general good, it is similarly ill advised to shoehorn the universal truth of human rights into every concrete situation. Using theatre to protect and promote human rights in often difficult circumstances invariably involves sensitive and sustained engagement with specific communities and contexts. As Sudhanva Deshpande of the Delhi-based theatre company Janam puts it in *Theatre of the Streets* (2007), the fact that street theatre entails 'a *density* of allusions and connections and associations' with its surroundings means it is both a driver and a product of 'fierce partisanship, a deep sense of solidarity with forces of progressive political change' (pp. 9–10, his emphasis). This is one of the reasons that (as some of the works listed in my 'Further reading' illustrate) critical accounts of these processes tend to be detailed and rich with description. But it is also instructive to note how often they begin with an account of how the theatre-makers had to adapt their preconceived ideas and strategies to the exigencies of the situation and the complications of locality.

For example, in analysing a prison theatre project in Brazil entitled *Staging Human Rights* (2004), Paul Heritage describes his initial shock when the State Secretary of

Prison Administration announced that many prison directors found 'human rights' to be a 'disgusting phrase': 'Sitting
beside him on the platform and waiting for my turn to
speak, I realise I have always assumed that the commonality
and equality of certain rights are the starting point for any
program or discussion. Here that is not the case' (p. 97).
As Heritage goes on to demonstrate, how he resolved the
tensions between his preconceptions and the situation he
found himself in – and how his collaborators reconciled
themselves to his intentions – then became integral to the
project as a whole.

This integration of ideals and actuality is a common pat-
tern in participatory human rights work, one that often
provides the narrative arc of the resulting critical reflections. It is nicely captured in the title of James Thompson's
book *Applied Theatre: Bewilderment and Beyond* (2003), but
the question then arises as to what, in the larger scheme of
things, the nature of that 'beyond' might be. There is always
scope for developing the relationship between theatre and
human rights in more nuanced and perceptive ways. But
whether the route taken is Crimp's cautionary interweaving
or Heritage and others' tentative integration, an essence or
perfect synthesis will always prove elusive. In part, this is
because theatre is a messy business, irremediably muddled
up in the world. But it is also because, despite the gargan-
tuan labour of abstraction upon which theories are built and
laws are worded, 'human rights' is a messy business too,
and this is the second reason for thinking about them in a
complementary relation to theatre. At ground level, there is

no such thing as a 'pure' human rights violation, or, indeed, rights-respecting system. The circumstances, motivations, actions and interpretations that make up any such event or environment are always multiple and invariably contradictory. Institutionally, the scope and weight of human rights is hotly contested, even in the case of a document as widely ratified as the Universal Declaration. By way of illustration, a preliminary list of quibbles about points already made in this study would include the following. Philosophically, the adequacy of 'dignity' – or indeed any other quality, essential or otherwise – as the basis of human rights is far from resolved. Legally, the Declaration was more aspirational than binding, and in some cases remains so. Logically, the Declaration includes different kinds of rights, some of which can lay a claim to cross-cultural consensus, whereas others are specific to the context of their formulation. Historically, its predominance risks privileging one story about rights at the expense of many others, both more ancient and more recent. Theoretically, conservatives bristle at the constraints human rights culture places on the individual, leftwing analysts believe it underplays socio-economic factors, and poststructuralists disagree with the underlying presumption of a rational and autonomous subject. Politically, the 'new' UN Human Rights Council remains as much a manifestation of *realpolitik* as of humankind's noblest sentiments. Rhetorically, the gap between what some states say and what they do in the name of human rights appears to be widening. Morally, how are we to credit an Arab charter ratified by the likes of Sudan (widely accused of orchestrating genocide in the Darfur region) or an ASEAN mechanism to which the repressive junta of Burma/Myanmar is party? And practically, what more can we say but that violence and oppression continue, in some places unabated, and in others, apace? Sometimes, the field of human rights can seem, well, all too human.

Given the contentiousness of the debate over the nature, function and place of human rights, it is not enough for us to know how theatre promotes or exercises those rights. Rather, we must use our knowledge of theatre to understand what human rights mean and what holding them entails.

In so doing, we are able to understand the practices both of theatre and of human rights in a more dynamic and less predetermined relationship. With regards to human rights, this allows a perspective that is at once more sanguine and more critical. One of the risks of viewing human rights solely through the prism of theatre is that the defining immediacy of the latter obscures the necessarily gradual evolution of the former. Of course, such progress is neither even nor assured. But if we are to take the universality of at least some basic rights seriously, we do their inalienability no favours by overstating their vulnerability (as, I would suggest, Harold Pinter came close to doing when he described dignity as 'so nearly lost to us' in his Nobel lecture).

For its part, de-linking theatre from the assumption that it must either promote or reactively 'problematise' human rights frees it up to pursue a parallel enquiry whose outcomes may be productively at odds with some of the basic assumptions behind the modern idea of human rights. The status of the body; the nature of subjectivity and intersubjectivity; the relationship between the individual and the state; the psychologically complex and sometimes self-destructive dynamics of suffering, oppression, need and desire; cultural memory, especially as an embodied practice; human relationships, especially as they emerge through dialogue and social participation; our continuing dependency on the non-human world; that crazy little thing called love – these are some of the central problems of the human condition that theatrical processes and performances of all kinds tussle with. 'Human rights' offers one noble and rather ingenious response: the strength of the theatre lies in the opportunities it affords to interrogate the basic conditions within which those rights must be anchored and, where they do not hold, to envision alternatives.

In what follows, I present three different ways of thinking theatre and human rights. For reasons of brevity, I stay fairly close to the topic at hand, considering first the role of performance in legal redress, then the light that theatre sheds on debates over the cultural specificity of rights, and finally an alternative take on human dignity in one of the best-known plays of the last century. In practice, the same approach should be possible even where theatre and human rights are more finely braided together, be it thinking through the relationship between violence and morality in a controversial play such as Sarah Kane's *Blasted* (1995), or between responsibilities and duties in risky and physically demanding body art, or between democracy and coercion in a community theatre project.

Paralegal performance

Throughout the second half of the twentieth century, the tenor and focus of international human rights discourse was overwhelmingly legalistic. Insofar as legislation is a key means of securing human rights, this is understandable, but it should not blind us to the personal and political dimensions both of human rights *and* of the law. In this section, I outline some of the ways theatre has intersected with legal frameworks, sometimes shoring them up, sometimes taking them to task. Using a term that usually designates some form of auxiliary contribution to legal processes, I describe these diverse events and practices as 'paralegal performance'.

For the Italian political philosopher Noberto Bobbio, the Universal Declaration inaugurated an 'Age of Rights', in which, as he wrote in 1967, 'for the first time in history a system of fundamental principles for human behaviour has been freely and expressly accepted by the majority of the people living on this planet through their governments' (*The Age of Rights*, pp. 14–15). In other words, all members of humanity could now justifiably claim to be citizens of the world, although, as history has since demonstrated, this did not mean world citizenship would take the same form as national belonging. In part, this is because of the historically contingent nature even of universal human rights; for Bobbio, the Declaration was a milestone in an ongoing process of emancipation whose character would continue to alter in response to changing social, economic and political conditions. But it is also because of the nature both of the

Declaration, which Bobbio described as 'something more than a doctrinal system, but something less than a system of legal norms' (p. 17), and of the modern nation-state. The fact is that even though many of the rights enshrined in the Declaration would subsequently be expanded and refined by legally binding international and regional instruments, the onus has remained overwhelmingly on individual states for their implementation (as when the United Kingdom passed the Human Rights Act in 1998, in accordance with the European Convention on Human Rights). In contrast, the relatively small number of rights bodies with international jurisdiction – such as the International Criminal Court – are notoriously limited in their powers.

The varying willingness and ability of governments to honour their international commitments is one reason for the unevenness of the human rights landscape globally, and a substantial challenge to local advocacy groups and to international bodies such as the United Nations. But enacting and enforcing domestic legislation is not the be-all and end-all of human rights protection. So-called customary law, for instance, provides a means of arguing rights cases on the basis of internationally accepted norms. It also points to the role of custom and practice in the evolution of the law, and here we can identify a point of intersection with a range of theatre practices.

In linguistics, a performative utterance is a *saying* which, under appropriate circumstances, is also a *doing*: it accomplishes the thing it describes. 'I sentence you to ...' is one such; 'I declare ...' another. Part of the ambiguity about the status of the Universal Declaration identified by Bobbio lies in its performative nature. *Proclaimed* by the General Assembly of the UN, the preamble exhorted 'every individual and every organ of society' to 'strive by teaching and education to promote respect for these rights and freedoms and by progressive measures, national and international, to secure their universal and effective recognition and observance'. Deriving its initial authority from the General Assembly's proclamation, the Declaration nevertheless acknowledged that its authority was neither definitive nor all-encompassing, and instead required the continuous enactment and reiteration of its principles.

Two long-term UK-based performance projects have taken the Declaration at its proclamatory word. In *rightsrepeated* (2005 onwards), performance artist Monica Ross, who has memorised a gender-neutral version of the document, proclaims it on invitation in diverse public venues. Meanwhile, the collective Leibniz have gradually been copying out the Declaration in their leather-bound *Book of Blood* (2006 onwards), inviting members of the public to add a single letter by donating a drop of blood. Both works are used as catalysts for additional activities: Ross has made available a poster version of her text, for use in other events, and each inscription of the *Book of Blood* is framed as a focal point for local artists and community groups to create their own rights-related works. The result is theatre that acts upon the requirement to disseminate the Declaration, while inviting members of the public to make their own commitment to its principles and highlighting the performative means by which it may achieve 'recognition and observance'.

In a sense, however, this is only the most literal of the ways theatre relates to an international human rights culture increasingly characterised by paralegal initiatives. In numerous societies, commissions, inquiries and reports are being used not so much to secure justice as to restore it where it has failed – and these formats are echoed in a range of performances.

An example is the rise of so-called tribunal theatre, which is closely – though not exclusively – associated in Britain with the work of 'editor' Richard Norton-Taylor and director Nicolas Kent at London's Tricycle Theatre. Performances typically reconstruct abbreviated versions of actual legal proceedings. In so doing, they tap into age-old formal correspondences between theatre and the law court, though they are a far cry from the mass media genres of courtroom drama or 'Court TV'. Instead, they stage verbatim (albeit in truncated form) either exceptional criminal trials such as *Nuremberg* and *Srebrenica* (both 1996) or, as in *The Colour of Justice: The Stephen Lawrence Inquiry* (1999) and *Bloody Sunday: Scenes from the Saville Inquiry* (2005), judicial procedures that ensued where, despite an inability to secure individual convictions, the social and/or political consensus determined that a wider case remained to be answered.

This public-interest dimension to the source material is key. We are reminded that human rights work often takes place where domestic legal provisions have been exhausted, which in turn suggests an intriguing ambiguity about what that 'work' consists in. For instance, the Stephen Lawrence inquiry, which in 1999 investigated why London's Metropolitan Police had failed to secure a conviction in a racially motivated murder case, provided at least three different opportunities for human rights issues to be addressed. First, following the collapse of their civil suit and a botched police inquiry into the original 1993 investigation, it provided an opportunity for the family of Stephen Lawrence to secure some form of moral, if not legal, redress. Second, the resulting report (known as the Macpherson Report) concluded that the Metropolitan Police were 'institutionally racist' and made a host of proposals to address the problem. And third, *The Colour of Justice* substantially extended both the event and the debate into the public domain. In part, this involved representing what happened during the inquiry. But when the actor playing the Assistant Commissioner of the Metropolitan Police apologises on its behalf to the actors playing Stephen Lawrence's parents ('Mr Lawrence, I wanted to say to you that I am truly sorry that we have let you down. It has been a tragedy for you. ... It has been a tragedy for the Metropolitan Police ...' [p. 128]), and when all stand for a minute's silence at the end, the performative force of the play lies not in its re-telling of what happened elsewhere but in what is collectively achieved by actors and audience in the theatre, at that moment.

In situations such as this, the practices of theatre and human rights overlap in the public performance both of testimony and of accountability. It is telling, however, that the Tricycle's *Called to Account: The Indictment of Anthony*

Charles Lynton Blair for the Crime of Aggression against Iraq – a Hearing (2007) is a more problematic play. Drawing on interviews with politicians, diplomats, weapons inspectors and other potential witnesses in the event that the former Prime Minister of the United Kingdom did actually face indictment for taking the country to war with Iraq in 2003, it rehearses the case both for and against the charge. However, this properly civil function of the theatre is somewhat undermined by the hypothetical nature of the enterprise; one cannot shake off the sense of wishful thinking that appears to sustain the play in the absence of any realistic possibility that such an event would come to pass. Used as a substitute for, rather than a supplement to, the law, the theatre is itself called to account – and, on the charge of misrecognising its significance, found wanting.

This is not to say that theatre can never perform such an interventionist function. Rather, as the Nigerian women's rights activist Mufuliat Fijabi makes clear in her report *A Mock Tribunal to Advance Change* (2004), it very much depends on the context. Held in 2001, the National Tribunal on Violence Against Women was a civil society initiative that aimed to highlight shortcomings in the law and public ignorance of such abuse. Thirty-three women and girls testified to their experiences of domestic and sexual violence before a panel of invited judges, who then retired to consider their verdict. Although the experiences recounted were true to life, and although the judges included senior figures from the legal profession and civil service, the testifiers had spent several days rehearsing, and the 'verdict' took the form of policy recommendations. The 2001 event was presented before an audience and local and international media. Its outcomes were used to put pressure on the government to respect international human rights commitments it had already signed up to. Fijabi concludes:

> By recreating this model [of a tribunal] on an informal level, the tactic simultaneously publi- cises the testimony and calls attention to existing gaps in government action. The need for a 'mock' tribunal automatically raises the question: 'Why isn't the state having its own tribunal?' (p. 14)

In other circumstances, it is the state itself that makes use of theatrical tactics, particularly when the focus is on restorative – rather than criminal – justice. Perhaps the best-known example of this is South Africa's Truth and Reconciliation Commission (TRC), which sat from 1996 to 1998 to investigate abuses committed between 1960 and 1994. It received widespread international coverage, not least because of striking television images which included the demonstration of torture techniques by victims and abusers, as well as emotional confrontations and apparently heartfelt pleas for amnesty and forgiveness. As that footage revealed, there was an element of theatricality in the set-up and structure of the hearings, and a performative element to establishing truth and fostering reconciliation.

On the tenth anniversary of the TRC, in 2006, these qualities were parlayed into *Truth in Translation*, a musical play derived from the experiences of the interpreters, who had provided simultaneous first-person translation during the hearings in eleven official languages. Conceived and directed by Michael Lessac, with music by Hugh Masekela, *Truth in Translation* opened with performances in Rwanda and South Africa, before touring to festivals and other post-conflict zones, such as Northern Ireland and Bosnia and Herzegovina. Supplemented by a post-show dialogue, educational materials, a photography exhibition and an extensive website, and with a documentary film in the pipeline, the performance can be seen as extending the lessons learnt by the TRC into the international arena.

In contrast, another South African performance, *Ubu and the Truth Commission* (Market Theatre, Johannesburg, 1997) by Jane Taylor, with William Kentridge and the Handspring Puppet Company, took the theatricality of the TRC as a spur to cross-examine the very process of reconciliation. Periodically, verbatim text from the TRC is used, 'spoken' in Zulu by witness puppets and translated into English. However, this strand of the play must contend with the chaotic world of the titular character, former policeman Pa Ubu. Memories of his violent past speak through fantastical creatures and perverse animation sequences, and his behaviour is by turns arrogant, abusive and self-pitying. Switching between unrepentant bluntness ('our Terror was no Reign of Error. We knew what we did, and still we did it' [p. 34]) and less-than-convincing expressions of remorse, Pa Ubu's strategic response to the TRC dramatises a tension in all such processes: that forgiveness comes more cheaply than redress. At the same time, the sheer excesses of the play – Pa Ubu's exaggerated grotesque, the proliferation of media, styles and references (not least to the anarchic source play, Alfred Jarry's *Ubu Roi* [1896]) – seem to make a wider point about the place of the TRC within the national psyche. Take, for instance, the following exchange:

> MA UBU: I see the prices are still rising.
> PA UBU: What uprising?
> MA UBU: Today, everything costs an arm and a leg.
> PA UBU: I had nothing to do with it!
> MA UBU: Pass me the salt.
> PA UBU: Who said it was assault! (p. 36)

Given what Pa Ubu has to hide, such paranoia is understandable. But the idea that accusations and judgments lie submerged within the most mundane interactions is one pursued throughout and cannot be reduced to a psychological tic of the patently guilty. Rather, the rhetoric of expiation and exculpation forms part of the play's general address and collectively implicates the audience in a past and a present that cannot be resolved by the personalisation of violence and suffering. Whereas truth commissions aim at the identification and clear separation of victims and oppressors, the play implies that the social body must absorb the full range of motivations, behaviours and experiences that are detailed, in all the complexity of their interrelations, and that moral judgements cannot fully encompass that range.

Where a key goal of many human rights advocates, then, is to see those rights enshrined in law, 'paralegal performance' names a more variegated field of activity. On the one hand, the performative dimension of human rights discourse, and the formal correspondences between theatre and court room, mean that theatre-makers are well placed to contribute to the practice of human rights promotion. This can involve supplementing the work of the law, and even acting as a temporary stand-in where legal provisions fall short. But it can also perform a more critical and sceptical function, drawing audiences back to aspects of the relationship between rights and responsibilities that are less easily adjudicated, particularly where theatricality may be an inherent part of the judicial process.

Theatre, culture and human rights

In 2002–3, a small number of complaints to the Malaysian authorities led to several theatre performances in the capital, Kuala Lumpur, encountering licensing difficulties. A series of perplexing about-turns followed, including a ban on the use of the word 'vagina' in two proposed re-stagings of the previously permitted *Vagina Monologues* and, following an outcry from artists and audience members, the *reversal* of a ban on the satirical company Instant Café Theatre. Where previously a synopsis had been sufficient to secure a licence, the Kuala Lumpur city council, DBKL, established a Script Evaluation Committee. As their guidelines, reproduced in Eddin Khoo *et al.*'s *Freedom of Expression in the Arts* (2003), put it, the aim was 'to ensure that performances are held in an atmosphere that is ethical and takes into consideration the interest of all parties and does not give rise to any uneasiness or feelings of unrest among individuals, agencies or organisations' (p. 118).

As in all situations where censorship is at issue, diverse factors were no doubt at play here, some political, some pragmatic, and some arbitrarily and obscurely personal. Nevertheless, aspects of the Malaysian case can be understood in wider reference to the universality of human rights. Like many modern nations, Malaysia was still a colony (the Federation of Malaya) when its British rulers signed up to the Universal Declaration in 1948. Postcolonial scepticism about the Enlightenment provenance of many features of human rights was almost inevitable. In the early 1990s, Malaysia joined other economically ascendant Asian countries in pressing for a shift in the international human rights agenda, in part on the cultural grounds that it did not accurately reflect so-called Asian values. While agreeing that human rights were universal in nature, these countries effectively managed to modify this universalism when they ensured that the Vienna Declaration of the World Conference on Human Rights (1993) placed the right to development on an equal footing with political rights and recognised that states could select standards for safeguarding rights on the basis of historical, religious and cultural particularities.

In Malaysia, these particularities include some history of tensions among its economically differentiated population of ethnic Malays, Chinese and Indians, who between them practise Islam, Buddhism, Hinduism and Christianity. Concern about offending any of these groups – particularly religious conservatives – is what lies behind the ostensibly innocuous reference to 'the interest of all parties' in the Script Evaluation Committee's guidelines. However, as is so often the case when states invoke local customs or conditions to justify restrictions on rights, it is necessary to ask which is the better served: justice and equality or political self-interest. Although Malaysian politicians have, in the past, accused Western governments of using human rights as a tool of political and economic domination, Malaysia has itself been criticised by human rights NGOs for politically motivated restrictions on civil liberties (including some, such as detention without trial, that are a colonial legacy).

Differentiating cultural bias and self interest from a contextually informed but disinterested approach to human rights is seldom easy. It is telling, however, that where 'culture' is invoked as a reason for compromising or critiquing human rights, it tends to refer to an idealised way of life rather than to creative expression. For example, proponents of 'Asian values' highlighted qualities such as thrift, strong families and respect for authority, but they had little to say about the importance traditionally accorded to artistic and aesthetic practice within Asian philosophies. This omission points to the largely political and economic motivations behind such ostensibly 'culturalist' arguments. It is also notable that, where they feel their rights are being threatened in the name of the culture to which they belong, artists can prove eloquent opponents. In response to the establishment of the Script Evaluation Committee in Malaysia, an artists' petition to the council entitled 'Stringent Guidelines Equals

Censorship' (and reproduced in Khoo *et al*.'s book) directly rebutted the coercive communitarianism of the guidelines by stating: 'It is through speaking about our identity that we feel we belong – it is by encountering different opinions within our society, and recognizing that we remain united nevertheless, that we build a society that is vibrant, exciting and strong' (p. 121).

By taking a stand when rights are threatened, artists may act not solely or even primarily in the name of any supervening concept of 'universal values', but to reassert some of the internal differences that characterise all cultures and nations, however apparently homogeneous. In the Malaysian case, this was accompanied by a strategic appeal to national unity, and, properly contextualised, this dual approach to recognising what is distinctive while affirming what is common about cultural identities can make an important contribution to the as-yet (and perhaps perpetually) unfinished process of universalising human rights.

Moreover, in an age of international mobility – with artists increasingly travelling to tour, train or collaborate – this capacity for asserting multiplicity at the subnational level is equally significant in cross-cultural contexts, where different interpretations of rights can be shared, exchanged and communicated to diverse audiences.

It is easy to be naive: the universalist approach to intercultural theatre taken by major European directors, including Peter Brook, has been roundly criticised by writers such as Rustom Bharucha for economic exploitation and inattention to cultural specificity. Where these inequalities can be resolved or confronted, however, something else might be achieved. Theatre-making demands a working-through of actions, ideas and relationships that calls for intensified interpersonal engagement and a distilling of lived experience. It is this processual quality, and the qualities of this process, that can make theatre-makers adept at cultural negotiation. Although neither the practice nor the watching of theatre is inherently internationalist, we might at least say that numerous theatrical forms are predisposed to fostering an international perspective, thereby exploring both commonalities and faultlines that diplomacy on the one hand, and national interests on the other, tend to obscure.

Not all cross-cultural work addresses these issues directly – nor should it. One can become as abrasively caught up in difference as blinded by sameness, and the theatrical approaches to these challenges are accordingly diverse. But one distinctive area where these differences must be taken as a given is where international contributions seek to help a people or culture address the legacy of human rights abuses that may otherwise be overwhelming. This is a situation fraught with the ethical and moral risks of intervention and self-interest. At the same time, participants and spectators alike can find great value in the resulting work – though not necessarily of the same kind or for the same reasons.

In the case of Cambodia, for example, numerous artistic initiatives have sought to address the legacy of the Khmer Rouge genocide (1975–9), during which approximately a third of the population was murdered, including 80 per cent of the country's performing artists. Foreign funds have contributed significantly to the long-term process of recovering and transmitting the complex gestures, choreographies and narratives of Cambodian classical dance theatre. More recently, several international theatre-makers have collaborated with Cambodian artists to devise and tour contemporary work that reflects on these events.

In TheatreWorks' *The Continuum: Beyond the Killing Fields* (New Theatre, Yale University, 2001), directed by the Singaporean Ong Keng Sen, four traditional Cambodian performers, a Singaporean performer and a translator presented documentary video footage, anecdotes, dance and shadow puppetry to tell of the Cambodians' struggle to revive their art forms. As inquisitive outsider, Noorlina Mohamed, the English-speaking Singaporean, often mediated between the auditorium and the stage, a role doubled – and sometimes contradicted – by the translator. It was Noorlina's video footage that showed the Cambodians' pre-tour rituals, the transformation of a flyblown cowhide into a shadow puppet and a fruitless search through the archives of the notorious Tuol Sleng prison for records of a star pupil believed to have been executed there. At other times she played the interlocutor and student. In a particularly striking scene, she received precise hands-on assistance from two of the performers in executing a dance that was concurrently performed by a third. This simple exercise in collective, embodied knowledge transmission underscored both the fragility of cultural memory and the labour of its remembering. It also suggested that, where memories have been erased or repressed within a society, identities might be recovered or re-forged in representing aspects of that society to outsiders.

There are, however, instructive and humbling limits to this. Like *The Continuum*, *3 Years, 8 Months, 20 Days* (Esplanade Studio Theatre, Singapore, 2007), by the Cambodian company Amrita Performing Arts and Dutch director Annemarie Prins, featured personal stories by the performers – in this case three actresses in their forties – about their experiences during the Khmer Rouge period. The stories were a harrowing combination of the mundane and the murderous: all the actors suffered hardship, lost loved ones and remain troubled by guilt at having survived. But as the stories went on, I, as an audience member, felt I was intruding on feelings that were simply too private for public display and found myself increasingly detached. I was reminded that one of the most intractable legacies of totalitarian and genocidal regimes is the dissolution of personal/public boundaries and that trauma fragments the capacity for telling and interpreting stories. But the limits to the communicability of experience that both performances dramatised also seem to suggest that even a universal conception of human rights cannot be totalising: we can recognise abuse, but there are limits to our understanding of its motivations and consequences.

This may be one reason that even a widespread belief in the value of human dignity and proscriptions on genocide and arbitrary killing and torture is more concretely expressed in the number of signatories to the Universal Declaration and subsequent legal instruments than in any globally agreed-upon philosophical formulation. Even those most committed to human rights as a universal foundation for justice and human flourishing on a global scale admit that the designation is as much prescriptive as descriptive – *saying* they are universal is one way of *making* them so. One of the uneasy truths the theatre can reveal is that the saying has its own limits, and that blind spots and absences are an integral, if troubling, part of the making process.

Lucky me! The right to rights

Habit, as someone once said, is a great deadener, and the consensus view that Samuel Beckett's *Waiting for Godot* (Théâtre de Babylone, Paris, 1953) marked a turning point in Euro-American theatre's treatment of the human condition tends to obscure the particular conception of the human that it explores. The fact that the writing of the play (October 1948 to January 1949) coincided with the drafting and proclamation of the Universal Declaration points up how distinctive was the context of its creation, as well as providing something of a foil for its staging of human *in*dignity. As such, at the heart of perhaps the most famous play of 'the age of rights', I suggest, is a novel and challenging conception of the human.

Godot is not in any conventional sense a war play (or an anti-war play, for that matter), but the traumatic aftermath of the Second World War, and the subsequent convulsions of reconstruction across Europe, are arguably reflected in the thwarted efforts of Vladimir and Estragon to move on, failing as they so elaborately do to gain sufficient traction on the world of meanings and things. When Lucky enters, luggage-laden and leashed to the ringmaster-slave driver

Pozzo, the tramps must confront the additional challenge of relating to other people, an uphill task given their new companions' negligible relationship to that epithet. Pozzo initially identifies Vladimir and Estragon as human beings, and therefore 'of the same species' as himself (p. 19). However, his dehumanisation of Lucky ('Up pig!' [p. 20]) is brutal and thorough, and begs the question of what value, if any, accrues to the human species as such, as well as what, if anything, might distinguish it from other kinds of animal.

Pozzo is the first to imply that the biological fact of his existence may not be a sufficient basis for personhood when he concedes that his treatment of Lucky comes at some cost to himself: 'I am perhaps not particularly human. But who cares?' (p. 27). Faced with such a rank spectacle of cruelty and suffering, the tramps try to care. But words fail even loquacious Vladimir – 'To treat a man … like that … I think that … no … a human being … no … it's a scandal!' (p. 25) – though it is unclear whether it is a lack of empathy that obviates the appropriate language, or vice versa. Everybody loves a scandal, though, and Vladimir's outrage is constantly sidetracked by his appalled fascination at Lucky's complicity in his own treatment, apparently unwilling as he is to put down the bags. That he *has* a will is simultaneously asserted and nullified by Pozzo, who reasons that since Lucky has the right to make himself comfortable yet does not, it is because he wishes to impress Pozzo so as to be kept in employment.

The logic is perverse, but no more so than the situation. It is true, after all, that although Lucky may be lacking in will, he wields a kind of power. Pozzo's sophistry and related disputations with the tramps are largely generated to compensate for Lucky's muteness, which, in combination with his open wounds ('a running sore!' [p. 23]) and constant slobbering, renders his presence – and therefore the claim he has on the attentions of both characters and audience – all the more insistent. The tramps make repeated attempts to detect in Lucky qualities they can recognise as human, but they become increasingly tyrannical in the process. In the command that Lucky dance comes one of the play's most explicit references to the Holocaust, recalling as it does the death camp entertainments the executioners demanded of their inmates.

When, following the instruction 'Think, pig!' (p. 44), Lucky does finally speak, it takes the form of a logorrhoeic outpouring that throws even Pozzo's tenuous claim to subjectivity into sharp relief. But it is not nonsense. Lucky channels a world in chaos, where the usual reference points have come adrift and there is quite literally no 'I' to speak of. He is subdued, eventually, and in the uneasy truce that follows, the characters' interdependency becomes apparent. Even the following morning, after Pozzo and Lucky have left, the encounter becomes the primary means by which Vladimir and Estragon reconstruct their memory of the day. In turn, this enables them to deduce their consciousness of the new moment *as* a new moment.

When the pair return, the rope restraining Lucky is shorter, and Pozzo blind. The dependence of the master on the slave is now entire; falling, neither can help the other up,

and their predicament prompts the tramps to fancy themselves humanitarians: 'To all mankind they were addressed,
those cries for help still ringing in our ears! But at this place,
at this moment of time, all mankind is us, whether we like
it or not. Let us make the most of it, before it is too late!'
(p. 90). They fail, of course, distracted – a failure easily
passed off as run-of-the-mill absurdity. But perhaps there is
a more instructive reason.

In a 1949 article, subsequently incorporated into her
influential book *The Origins of Totalitarianism* (1966 [1951]),
the political philosopher Hannah Arendt identified in the
wartime plight of minorities and the stateless a fundamental
paradox in the conventional understanding of human rights.
Although supposedly grounded in the sovereignty of the
individual, and independent of any reference to an external
authority such as God or a feudal lord, human rights are,
she noted, precisely what one does *not* possess when one is a
'mere presence in the world' (p. 286), 'a human being and
nothing else' (p. 302). In contrast to the refugee, argued
Arendt, herself a German Jew who escaped to America
in 1941, even criminals are more meaningfully human,
because the state must recognise them as such in order to
punish them according to the law. She goes on:

> We became aware of the existence of a right to
> have rights (and that means to live in a frame-
> work where one is judged by one's actions and
> opinions) and a right to belong to some kind
> of organised political community, only when

> millions of people emerged who had lost and
> could not regain these rights because of the new
> global political situation. (pp. 296–7)

Although it is tempting, then, to see in Lucky a character who is deprived of rights by those around him, Arendt's analysis of the wider structural and political consequences of the Second World War suggests that Pozzo and the tramps are little better off. Lacking sufficient trappings of a social structure within which they might speak or act meaningfully – that is to say, in such a way as to make a material difference to their situation – none of the characters is able to exercise his 'right to rights'. Vladimir and Estragon's hope that Godot will appear is not, therefore, as quixotic as it may otherwise seem, as he represents not simply a figure of authority but a means by which they might measure their own way in the world. Their failure to be humane lies precisely in the fact that, as Vladimir puts it, 'all mankind is us'.

And yet the situation the play presents is not quite as hopeless as it might seem, because of course it *does* take place within a framework for judging actions and opinions – that of the theatrical event. 'At me too someone is looking,' says Vladimir (p. 105). It's a red herring for him but bait for us. While the characters struggle to identify sufficient value in each other to be recognised as human, the audience bears witness to their plight, and finds, in the poetry and the pratfalls, grounds on which to mark the characters as having *appeared*.

Estragon, in contrast, continues to harbour thoughts of revenge for a dimly remembered hurt visited upon him by Lucky the previous day. It is done in a flurry of kicks, though not before the revenger has sustained a further injury in the execution, enough to forestall any risk of novelty the following day. At the very least, the logic of this casual violence reminds us that the concept of the human and the rights that automatically follow from it may not be as self-evident as the drafters of the Universal Declaration believed them to be. A more active mode of recognition may be required. Meanwhile, Pozzo and Lucky shuffle off, and Vladimir reflects on the morrow: 'He'll know nothing. He'll tell me about the blows he received and I'll give him a carrot.' And then: 'We have time to grow old. The air is full of our cries. (*He listens.*) But habit is a great deadener' (pp. 104–5).

Part Three

theatres of cruelty

Summoned to perform

We have now examined what theatre can tell us about human rights, and how the two might be thought of in mutually informing terms. The conception of theatre that emerges is wide-ranging and complex, but one assumption that goes unquestioned in all the examples given is their right to take place at all.

Is this appropriate? What if performance itself were construed as an abuse of human rights? In my discussion of *Waiting for Godot*, for example, I argued that an audience's attempt to understand – or at least bear witness to – the characters' dilemmas itself provides a framework within which the world of the play might have meaning. But this cannot easily be disentangled from the much more troubling act of spectating that occurs when Lucky is ordered by the others to dance. There, the right to perform is reconfigured as the command to appear, a transformation that is violent in its initial enactment and cruel in its presentation before an audience.

The distinctive force of this dynamic was underlined in November 2004 when a human rights group filmed a Palestinian man playing his violin in front of Israeli soldiers at a West Bank checkpoint. The footage gained wide media attention, in part because, like Lucky's dance, it carried historical resonances of Jewish musicians forced to perform for their Nazi captors during the Second World War. The subsequent furore in 2004 centred on whether, after having asked Wissam Tayem to take his violin out of its case to show it did not contain explosives, the soldiers instructed him to play. Tayem claimed they had, and that they had requested 'something sad', but an Israeli Defence Force statement, despite censuring the soldiers for insensitivity, countered that he had done so 'of his own volition' (2004).

It would be fatuous to draw a direct parallel with theatre-making, but the ensuing debate over the will and agency of the 'performer' in the checkpoint case reminds us of the dynamics of power within the theatrical event. 'The show must go on' is usually muttered in wry resignation, as thespians gamely confront yet another hurdle to meeting the audience's demand that they appear as promised. But the never-say-die attitude that reinforces the image of the stage as an unimpeachably magical place of possibility can detract from the phrase's darker purpose. For in the imperative 'must' lurks an obligation to 'keep up appearances' that, given half the chance, will ride roughshod over labour laws, health and safety regulations and, in the case of demagogic directors and egotistical actors, basic human decency. Overall, the theatre experience involves a concatenation of desires, emotions, ideas and affects which lie in a highly ambiguous relationship to those actions and sentiments ideally at work in a rights-respecting scenario.

This, of course, is part of the theatre's appeal, as well as the basis for its sometimes troubling relationship with the world beyond the playing-space. Post-9/11 in particular, many kinds of theatre take place within a spectacular economy where the processes of staging and gazing have become inextricably linked with images of suffering and titillation. Theatre-makers of all persuasions have taken up the challenge to respond accordingly – particularly in relation to the politics, psychology and personal consequences of terrorism and counter-terrorism. For example, a representatively broad selection of performances dealing with the legal no man's land established by the United States at Guantánamo Bay Detention Camp in 2002 include Victoria Brittain and Gillian Slovo's *Guantánamo: Honor Bound to Defend Freedom* (Tricycle, London, 2004), which compiled speeches, transcripts and correspondence to depict the plight of four detainees; *Bare Life Study #1* (2005), where the performance artist Coco Fusco, dressed as a military policewoman, had fifty orange jumpsuit-clad volunteers clean the ground in front of the US Consulate in São Paolo, Brazil, with toothbrushes; *Honour Bound* (2006), a dance-theatre piece conceived and directed by Nigel Jamieson and choreographed by Gary Stewart for the Sydney Opera House and Malthouse Theatre, which focused on the detention of the Australian David Hicks; and annual cross-continental protests on 11 January by Amnesty International, whose members mark the first transfers of detainees to the camp by wearing orange jumpsuits and performing a series of drills depicting their plight.

These and similar performances can point to reviews, analyses and media coverage that confirm their success in rendering otherwise abstract injustices palpable and emotive. Individually, they can claim, as the battle cry has it, to have spoken truth to power. But if they are considered collectively, one is compelled to ask whether they spoke as eloquently as they might have done, and in what language. A number of tropes emerge across such works – the black hood and orange jumpsuit; the cage; the stress position; the crewcut guard; the juxtaposition of political evasion and physical suffering, of noble sentiments and sentimental pleading – that are instantly recognisable in the public imagination as the theatricalised trappings of the so-called War on Terror. But this very familiarity gives reason for pause. Is there not a limit to the insights that can be communicated when the aesthetic agenda is so comprehensively determined by what one is criticising? Surely, what is most challenging about such images is not that they show incriminating evidence of cruel and unusual treatments but that the system which produced them saw no contradiction in stating, as then-President George W. Bush did in a February 2008 interview with the BBC, 'We believe in human rights and human dignity. We believe in the human condition. We believe in freedom.'

In a global media environment that produces and exploits theatricalised suffering, the theatre is uniquely placed to

critique the use and fetishisation of such images and to provide a nuanced account of the ideology that produced them
in the name of human rights. However, fastening too tightly
on the images themselves risks not only an oversimplification of the issues but complicity with a system where political passions on all sides tend to drown out moral reflection,
symbolic gestures trump ethical action, and passion itself is
rendered partisan.

Indeed, although the readiness of a wide range of practitioners to denounce such abuses confirms the theatre in
one of its proper social functions, it may also raise a more
troubling possibility: that the very fact of theatrical appearance distorts our understanding of human rights and their
violations. Revelations in 2005 that America's Central
Intelligence Agency operated an international network of
'black sites' − secret prisons outside US jurisdiction where
suspected 'enemy combatants' were interrogated and in
some cases tortured − served as a reminder that the vast
majority of human rights abuses worldwide take place
behind closed doors and are characterised by some form of
disappearance.

Most literally, this involves the forcible removal of
individuals to a place of incarceration or, as in Argentina's
'Dirty War' in the 1970s and 1980s, execution. But arguably any form of silencing, whether by means of threat,
injunction or coercion, entails a form of disappearance,
even when the subject remains in plain sight. Indeed, one
way of thinking about the systematic suppression of human
rights is as a kind of wholesale limitation on what can be

thought or known: it may appear benign, precisely for the reason that an entire tranche of human experience is expunged from the social world.

Can theatre mark these disappearances, or does the spectacle conspire in a cover-up? The dichotomy is a false one, as appearance and disappearance are interdependent concepts and practices. A celebrated example of appearance being used to contest disappearance is the Mothers of the Plaza de Mayo organisation, which has used performative means since 1977 to protest weekly in central Buenos Aires against the loss of their children during the 'Dirty War'. Many cases, however, are less cut and dried. The spectacular appearance of the Guantánamo detainees, for example, was directly linked to a legal disappearance from the category 'human' (as well as, some might add, to the moral diminution of those in whose name such treatment was justified).

In this and many other cases, it is more important that the theatre mark the ways in which appearance and disappearance underwrite each other than that they resolve the ensuing tensions. To the extent that theatre-making is a process of problem-solving, this is easier said than done, although a useful closing example is offered by Lebanese artists Rabih Mroué, The Atlas Group and Walid Raad. In multimedia performances such as *Three Posters* (Smaha House, Beirut, 2000), which focused on the video testaments of suicide bombers, and *Looking for a Missing Employee* (Theatre Al-Madina, Beirut, 2003), which used media reports to reconstruct the disappearance of a government functionary, Mroué and his collaborators turned the theatre into a site where the boundaries between fact and fiction were irremediably blurred, and the truth value conventionally assigned to certain kinds of testimony and media presentation were called profoundly into question. In the lecture-performance *My Neck Is Thinner Than a Hair* (2001) by Walid Raad and The Atlas Group, the history of car-bombing in Beirut was presented in authoritative PowerPoint format, with contextualising digressions into Lebanese history, politics and culture, some provided apparently ad hoc in response to questions from the audience. When I watched the 'performance', only gradually did it dawn on me that the dense networks of facts, figures and analyses were tied by strands of fabrication and that the questioners in the audience were 'plants'. By the end, I felt affronted that they had taken advantage of my ignorance of the situation in Lebanon and had betrayed my faith in them to be straight with me.

Of course, this was the lesson I needed to learn. Given the carnage that has been visited upon Lebanon since the 1970s, the artists' refusal to flag up what was 'real' and what 'fake' in their presentation could not be shrugged off as a glib postmodern game of competing truth claims. Rather, it indicates that where history is obscure, violence endemic, the media compromised, memory suppressed and (as in the case of car-bombing) evidence destroyed even as it is produced, new ways must be found of responding to and representing the past. The theatre, with its questionable relationship to truth, may paradoxically represent one of the best venues for pursuing such a strategy. In contrast to the pieces about Guantánamo, which both respond to and re-enact the violent moment of spectacularisation, these Lebanese works reproduce situations where violence became endemic, and therefore mundane. By this token, the orange jumpsuit is a red herring. The theatre can properly respond to such abuses only when they have been de-theatricalised: it is most effective where least expected, most creative where least brutally affirmed.

Conclusion: unaccommodated man

How, then, to conclude? Sometimes, the narrative closure of books, like the literal or metaphorical curtain at the end of a performance, can distract us from the open-endedness of as vast and ambitious a project as that of promoting and protecting human rights. The fact is that there is no one-to-one correspondence between 'Theatre' and 'Human Rights', and identifying the ways that the former serves, complements or offsets the latter requires ongoing vigilance on the part of practitioners, audiences and critics alike. If we were able to gather up the diverse events and practices covered in this book and ask what theatre thinks of human rights today, the answer is less likely to be blind advocacy than a strategic combination of vocal support, provisional consensus and robust scepticism.

In lieu of a homily, then, I would like to offer one last example of 'thinking theatre and human rights' that prompts some observations about the future development of human rights culture, as well as theatre's relationship to it.

During the famous storm scene in Shakespeare's play, we find King Lear 'unbonnetted' (both of crown and hat), turned out of his daughters' houses and pummelled by the elements. His arrogance and foolishness laid bare, he encounters a vagrant, Poor Tom, and sees in him a kindred spirit: 'unaccommodated man is no more but such a poor, bare, forked animal as thou art' (III.4.103–4). Making to undress in sympathy, Lear turns a corner in his understanding of his place in the world and the consequences of his actions – and the audience, too, is provided with a striking vision of human life stripped to its most basic and elemental properties.

Although in one regard the storm is a manifestation of Lear's inner turmoil, as the Gentleman tells Kent, its scale and ferocity far outstrip 'his little world of man' (III.1.10). Lear is humbled not only because of arrogance towards his family and subjects but because of hubris in the face of nature. The lowliness of the hovel where he finds shelter shows how far he has fallen, and also how insignificant even the powerful are when set against the world at large.

Watching the play in the age of El Niño, the Indian Ocean tsunami of 2004, and 2005's Hurricane Katrina, one is reminded how little a concern with human rights may amount to if they are not placed in their properly global context. Like latter-day Lears (subsequently, he prays for those exposed to the storm and berates himself for ignoring their plight in the past), we are becoming increasingly aware that poverty, resource scarcity and ecocide are linked to human dignity in ways that oblige a rethinking of the individualistic basis of traditional human rights. Indeed, one might go so far as to note that the anthropocentric underpinnings of Enlightenment humanism may be one of the greatest impediments to the universalisation of 'human' rights. Certainly, other world philosophies and religions take a more balanced view of humankind's relationship to the environment and indeed the cosmos, and although this by no means guarantees greater protection for the species or the world, it may provide an *intellectual* resource for rethinking the scope of our responsibilities.

Far from being an eco-fable, however, the storm scene in *King Lear* also draws attention to questions about the distinctiveness of 'man'. Naked and cold, Poor Tom describes himself living an animal existence, his encounters with other people resulting in his being whipped, put in the stocks, banished or imprisoned. At first, Lear rather comically presumes Tom must also have suffered at the hands of unkind daughters. Gradually, however, it dawns on him that despite his earlier claim that even beggars 'are in the poorest thing superfluous' (II.4.260) (meaning that everyone has more than their needs), Tom is 'the thing itself' (III.4.103), the other of Lear, Kent and the Fool, whose very clothing, however ragged, renders them 'sophisticated' (III.4.102) by comparison.

There are echoes here of Hannah Arendt's description of the 'abstract nakedness' of the merely human upon which, she claimed, the Rights of Man are both founded and founder. Writing in the post-9/11 context, the philosopher Judith Butler has developed this analysis. In *Precarious Life* (2004), she states:

> The public sphere is constituted in part by what can appear, and the regulation of the sphere of

> appearance is one way to establish what will
> count as reality, and what will not. It is also a
> way of establishing whose lives can be marked
> as lives, and whose deaths will count as deaths.
> (pp. xx–xxi)

Butler is wary of presuming 'a common notion of the human' (p. 31), but nevertheless argues the importance of attempting to fathom its possibility, on the basis not of the discriminations that have resulted in the carnage of so-called humanitarian intervention but of human beings' common vulnerability to each other.

Although the future of human rights may lie in rethinking their relationship to the environment in less species-centric terms, then, the category of 'human' must be defended against those who consider that some people are more human than others. As a heightened experience of human co-presence, meaning-making and imagining, the theatre presents itself as a useful site for addressing this challenge. But is this not somewhat at odds with Butler's contention that our concerns should be with what *cannot* appear? Lear attempts to become 'the thing itself' by giving his clothes to Tom. Yet not only would this do little to change the situation fundamentally, as he would thereby relinquish the last vestiges of his sovereignty, only to become subject to someone else's, but the very act of choosing automatically compromises the gesture by rendering it inherently in excess of 'the thing itself'.

How, in other words, can the theatre explore what is excluded from the designation 'human' when the very process of staging something serves to reaffirm the human as it is already understood? There is no easy answer to this question – but there is a paradox we might usefully learn to live with. Let us not forget that Lear's 'moment of truth' is born of deception, because Tom is in fact Gloucester's son Edgar. His life at risk following his half-brother's treachery, Edgar bases his disguise on the beggars he has seen roaming the countryside. He tells the audience that his will be a 'presented nakedness' (II.3.11), and later, during Lear's fake trial of his daughters, confesses that he is so touched by the old man's plight, his tears 'mar my counterfeiting' (III.6.60).

I propose that there is a theatrical truth to this paradox – whereby theatricality and dissimulation throw into relief qualities of 'the thing itself' that are otherwise difficult to imagine and impossible to represent. Or, to put it another way, to the extent that the theatre provides a partial refuge from the real, it can sharpen audience members' sensitivity to the consequences of human exposure. Perhaps this is one of the reasons that, far from being unique to *King Lear*, the figure of the unaccommodated man wanders through many plays and performances – just as he does through this book, in the guise of Polynices in *Antigone*, Boal's 'Joker', Lucky in *Godot*, Mroué's missing employee – unaccommodated, as it were, by any of them, but nevertheless activating a productive theatrical tension.

Needless to say, the figure of the unaccommodated *man* enacts its own exclusions. Vulnerability, as Butler puts it, is differentiated, and allocated differentially across the globe.

To take only the broadest such distinctions, women and, in other ways, children not only have different experiences of exposure and vulnerability but experience these phenomena differently. More work remains to be done on the precise nature of their unaccommodation arrangements.

In closing, however, I do wonder whether the unaccommodated man, as well as being a theatrical figure, may not also be one way of figuring the theatre itself. I could not help but recall Lear's search for shelter as I travelled across Singapore in July 2007 to watch a forum theatre performance by local company Drama Box. *Trick or Threat* was a multilingual performance in Malay, Mandarin and English which focused on inter-ethnic tensions in the context of a bomb threat on the underground system. The event itself combined many of the joys and limitations of forum theatre: fascinating polyglot, cross-ethnic, cross-gender participation from the 'spect-actors', but also an oversimplification of race relations on the part of both audience members and theatre-makers.

What was particularly interesting about *Trick or Threat*, however, was that it took place at all. Drama Box had originally applied for a licence to perform outdoors in the Chinatown area of central Singapore. This was refused by the authorities on the grounds that an outdoor event dealing with the 'sensitive' issue of 'race' could prove inflammatory. The fact that the performance specifically sought to address and ameliorate inter-ethnic tensions was immaterial. Convinced that their core constituency of passers-by and non-theatre-goers would be alienated by a stipulation that the performance must take place indoors, Drama Box eventually reached a compromise with the authorities, and *Trick or Threat* took place in a distant suburb of the city-state, in a marquee erected between a shopping mall and a community centre.

Singapore is more authoritarian than most developed nations; nevertheless I find in that tent a resonantly ambivalent image with which to close this book. Drama Box created theatre both in and as a temporary shelter. They did so in order to pose questions about a pressing challenge both to human life and to human rights. Yet to explore answers that would not otherwise get an airing, they had to curtain the process from view: neither consumerism in the mall nor civic participation at the community centre could be troubled. In this combination of possibility and compromise, the theatre's unaccommodations — both to human rights culture and to human rights abuses — are made apparent. As the unaccommodated man Antonin Artaud put it in *The Theatre and Its Double* (1970 [1936]), in a line that seems to renew itself with each new atrocity and each new triumph of the modern age, 'We are not free and the sky can still fall on our heads. And above all else, theatre is made to teach us this' (p. 60).

further reading

A wealth of information about human rights exists in published and online forms. The United Nations has extensive web resources devoted to the topic, and the United Nations Educational, Scientific and Cultural Organization (UNESCO) site is useful for information on cultural rights. The University of Minnesota Human Rights Library is the most comprehensive online resource for international human rights instruments, but for a snapshot of the contemporary human rights situation, visit the sites of the major NGOs, which include Amnesty International, Human Rights Watch, and Freedom House. All publish freely accessible annual reports. NGOs focusing specifically on freedom of expression and civil liberties include Article 19, International PEN and Index on Censorship. These sites include extensive links to other organisations. Finally, Open Democracy provides a good example of how rights issues inform the broader current affairs agenda.

In terms of print publications, *The Essentials of Human Rights* (2005), edited by Rhona Smith and Christien van den Anker, provides short overviews of many topics, but the dryness of the writing does not encourage one to linger; better to move swiftly on to Susan Marks and Andrew Clapham's *International Human Rights Lexicon* (2005), which offers a nuanced and expansive exploration of key themes. In turn, Liam Gearon's *The Human Rights Handbook* (2003) and *Freedom of Expression and Human Rights* (2006) accessibly collate key documents, ideas and resources, and two books by Micheline Ishay – the edited volume *The Human Rights Reader* (1997) and her *History of Human Rights* (2004) – provide plenty of context for entering the choppy waters of human rights theory. The most comprehensive overview to date of key concepts and debates is provided by Richard Falk *et al.*'s five-volume compendium *Human Rights: Critical Concepts in Political Science* (2008), although, as the subtitle indicates, not everything will be of equal interest: focus on volumes 1 and 4. As for book-length studies, Darren O'Byrne's *Human Rights: An Introduction* (2003) is wide-ranging and accessible, and James Nickel's *Making Sense of Human Rights* (2007) and Jack Donnelly's *Universal Human Rights in Theory and Practice* (2003) provide overviews while developing their own arguments, the latter with a focus on the question of cultural specificity. Critical perspectives on human rights are to be found in Joanne R. Bauer and Daniel A. Bell's *The East Asian Challenge for Human Rights* (1999), Makau Mutua's *Human Rights* (2002) and Carl Wellman's *The Proliferation of Rights* (1999): see below for their self-explanatory subtitles.

Meanwhile, the 2004 special issue of the journal *South Atlantic Quarterly* edited by Ian Balfour and Eduardo Cadava is a difficult but essential collection of essays critiquing the humanist individualism of mainstream human rights discourse. The Oxford Amnesty Lectures, detailed online and published annually since 1992, are consistently provocative, nuanced and culturally insightful, and, for a breath of fresh air, Walter Kälin *et al.*'s *The Face of Human Rights* (2004) combines an excellent introductory essay with a panoramic collection of rights-related images.

Few books focus solely on theatre and human rights, because these subjects are usually subsumed into other categories or approaches. Hence, there are discussions of human rights-related material in Petra Kuppers', Eugène van Erven's, and Richard Boon and Jane Plastow's books on community theatre and theatre for development; Tim Prentki and Sheila Preston's, James Thompson's and Helen Nicholson's books on applied drama (the latter includes a valuable chapter on human rights); van Erven's and Jan Cohen-Cruz's books on protest theatre; and Will Hammond and Dan Steward's edited volume *Verbatim Verbatim* (2007). Catherine Cole analyses the performative dimension of South Africa's Truth and Reconciliation process in *Stages of Transition* (2009), and Julie Holledge and Joanne Tompkins discuss the Mothers of the Plaza de Mayo in their *Women's Intercultural Performance* (2000). Explorations of theatre, ecology and animality can be found in books by Alan Read and Baz Kershaw and in a 2007 special issue of *The Drama Review* edited by Una Chaudhuri. Although there is something of an emphasis on

Southeast Asia in the present study, the books listed below by Coco Fusco, Guillermo Gomez-Peña and Diana Taylor provide much fascinating and often entertaining material with a focus on the Americas. The New Tactics website features 'tactical notebooks' outlining the use of theatre for rights activism. Perhaps because of the specificity such enquiries require, some of the most interesting resources on participatory theatre are to be found in journals rather than books. These include issues of *Research in Drama Education* and *The Drama Review*. It is also worth noting that many of the artists' websites listed below include links to other resources.

Human rights and human rights theory

Amnesty International. Freedom of Expression Award. 30 June 2008 <http://www.amnesty.org.uk/content.asp?CategoryID=10926>.

Arendt, Hannah. *The Origins of Totalitarianism*. 1951. Rev. ed. London: Allen & Unwin, 1966.

Balfour, Ian, and Eduardo Cadava, eds. *And Justice for All? The Claims of Human Rights*. Spec. iss. of *South Atlantic Quarterly* 103.2/3 (2004).

Bauer, Joanne R., and Daniel A. Bell, eds. *The East Asian Challenge for Human Rights*. Cambridge: Cambridge UP, 1999.

Bobbio, Norberto. *The Age of Rights*. 1990. Trans. Allan Cameron. Cambridge: Polity, 1996.

Bush, George W. 'In Full: George W. Bush's BBC Interview.' 14 Feb. 2008. BBC News. 15 Feb. 2008 <http://news.bbc.co.uk/2/hi/americas/7245670.stm>.

Butler, Judith. *Precarious Life: The Powers of Mourning and Violence*. London and New York: Verso, 2004.

Donnelly, Jack. *Universal Human Rights in Theory and Practice*. 2nd ed. Ithaca, NY, and London: Cornell UP, 2003.

Falk, Richard, Hilal Elver, and Lisa Hajjar, eds. *Human Rights: Critical Concepts in Political Science*. 5 vols. Abingdon, UK, and New York: Routledge, 2008.

Gearon, Liam. *The Human Rights Handbook: A Global Perspective for Education*. Stoke on Trent and Sterling, UK: Trentham, 2003.

————. *Freedom of Expression and Human Rights: Historical, Literary and Political Contexts*. Brighton, UK, and Portland, OR: Sussex Academic Press, 2006.

Hegel, G. W. F. *Phenomenology of Spirit*. 1807. Trans. A. V. Miller. Oxford: Clarendon, 1977.

Israeli Defence Force. *Findings of the Investigation regarding the Incident of the Palestinian Playing a Violin at a Checkpoint Near Nablus*. 30 Nov. 2004. 15 Feb. 2008 <http://www.imra.org.il/story.php3?id=23001>.

Ishay, Micheline R., ed. *The Human Rights Reader: Major Political Writings, Essays, Speeches, and Documents from the Bible to the Present*. London and New York: Routledge, 1997.

————. *The History of Human Rights: From Ancient Times to the Globalization Era*. Berkeley: U of California P, 2004.

Kälin, Walter, Lars Müller, and Judith Wyttenbach, eds. *The Face of Human Rights*. Baden, Switzerland: Lars Müller, 2004.

Landman, Todd. *Studying Human Rights*. London and New York: Routledge, 2006.

Marks, Susan, and Andrew Clapham. *International Human Rights Lexicon*. Oxford: Oxford UP, 2005.

Mutua, Makau. *Human Rights: A Political and Cultural Critique*. Philadelphia: U of Pennsylvania P, 2002.

Nickel, James W. *Making Sense of Human Rights*. 2nd ed. Oxford: Blackwell, 2007.

O'Byrne, Darren J. *Human Rights: An Introduction*. Harlow, UK: Longman, 2003.

Smith, Rhona K. M., and Christien van den Anker, eds. *The Essentials of Human Rights*. London and New York: Hodder Arnold, 2005.

UNESCO. 'Appendix B: Principles and Guidelines for the Protection of the Heritage of Indigenous Peoples.' *Cultural Rights and Wrongs*. Ed. Halina Nieć. Paris and Leicester, UK: UNESCO and Institute of Art and Law, 1998. 198–202.

United Nations. Universal Declaration of Human Rights. 10 Dec. 1948. 10 Dec. 2007 <http://www.un.org/Overview/rights.html>.

Waldron, Jeremy, ed. *Nonsense upon Stilts: Bentham, Burke and Marx on the Rights of Man*. London and New York: Methuen, 1987.

Wellman, Carl. *The Proliferation of Rights: Moral Progress or Empty Rhetoric?* Boulder, CO: Westview, 1999.

Theatre books, journals and plays

Akand, Motahar. *Action Theatre: Initiating Changes*. Minneapolis, MN: Center for Victims of Torture New Tactics for Human Rights Project, 2007. 4 Jan. 2009 <http://www.newtactics.org/en/ ActionTheatre>.

Anderson, Patrick, and Jisha Menon, eds. *Violence Performed: Local Roots and Global Routes of Conflict*. Houndmills, UK: Palgrave Macmillan, 2008.

Artaud, Antonin. *The Theatre and Its Double*. 1936. Trans. Victor Corti. London: Calder and Boyars, 1970.

Beckett, Samuel. *Waiting for Godot*. New York: Grove, 1954.

Bharucha, Rustom. *Theatre and the World: Performance and the Politics of Culture*. London and New York: Routledge, 1993.

————. *The Politics of Cultural Practice: Thinking Through Theatre in an Age of Globalization*. London: Athlone, 2000.

Boal, Augusto. *Theater of the Oppressed*. 1974. Trans. Charles A. and Maria-Odilia Leal McBride. New York: Urizen, 1979.

————. *The Rainbow of Desire: The Boal Method of Theatre and Therapy*. Trans. Adrian Jackson. London and New York: Routledge, 1995.

————. *Legislative Theatre: Using Performance to Make Politics*. 1996. Trans. Adrian Jackson. London and New York: Routledge, 1998.

Boon, Richard, and Jane Plastow, eds. *Theatre and Empowerment: Community Drama on the World Stage*. Cambridge: Cambridge UP, 2004.

Brittain, Victoria, and Gillian Slovo. *Guantánamo: 'Honor Bound to Defend Freedom'*. London: Oberon, 2004.

Chaudhuri, Una, ed. *Animals and Performance*. Spec. iss. of *The Drama Review* 51.1 (2007).

Cohen-Cruz, Jan, ed. *Radical Street Performance: An International Anthology*. London and New York: Routledge, 1998.

Cole, Catherine. *Stages of Transition: Performing South Africa's Truth Commission*. Bloomington: Indiana UP, 2009.

Crimp, Martin. *Plays 2*. London: Faber & Faber, 2005.

Deshpande, Sudhanva, ed. *Theatre of the Streets: The Jana Natya Manch Experience*. Delhi: Jana Natya Manch, 2007.

Dorfman, Ariel. *The Resistance Trilogy: Widows, Death and the Maiden, Reader*. London: Nick Hern, 1998.

Fijabi, Mufuliat. *A Mock Tribunal to Advance Change*. Minneapolis, MN: Center for Victims of Torture New Tactics for Human Rights Project, 2004. 4 Jan. 2009 <http://www.newtactics.org/en/AMockTribunaltoAdvanceChange>.

Fusco, Coco, ed. *Corpus Delecti: Performance Art of the Americas*. London and New York: Routledge, 1999.

———. *The Bodies That Were Not Ours: And Other Writings*. London and New York: Routledge, 2001.

———. *Field Guide for Female Interrogators*. New York: Seven Stories, 2008.

Gilbert, Helen, and Sophie Nield, eds. *Performance and Asylum*. Spec. iss. of *Research in Drama Education* 13.2 (2008).

Gomez-Peña, Guillermo. *Ethno-Techno: Writings on Performance, Activism and Pedagogy*. London and New York: Routledge, 2005.

Groupov. *Rwanda 94*. Brussels: Carbon 7, 2001.

Hammond, Will, and Dan Steward, eds. *Verbatim Verbatim: Techniques in Contemporary Documentary Theatre*. London: Oberon, 2007.

Heritage, Paul. 'Taking Hostages: Staging Human Rights.' *The Drama Review* 48.3 (2004): 96–106.

Holledge, Julie, and Joanne Tompkins. *Women's Intercultural Performance*. London and New York: Routledge, 2000.

Kershaw, Baz. *Theatre Ecology: Environments and Performance Events*. Cambridge: Cambridge UP, 2008.

Khoo, Eddin, Ramdas Tikamdas, and Elizabeth Wong, eds. *Freedom of Expression in the Arts*. Kuala Lumpur: National Human Rights Society (HAKAM), 2003.

Kuppers, Petra. *Community Theatre: An Introduction*. London and New York: Routledge, 2007.

Madison, D. Soyini, and Judith Hamera, eds. *The SAGE Handbook of Performance Studies*. Thousand Oaks, CA: SAGE, 2006.

Nicholson, Helen. *Applied Drama: The Gift of Theatre*. Houndmills, UK: Palgrave Macmillan, 2005.

Nobel Foundation. 'The Nobel Prize in Literature 2005.' Press release, 13 Oct. 2005. 7 Dec. 2007 <http://nobelprize.org/nobel_prizes/literature/laureates/2005/press.html>.

Norton-Taylor, Richard. *The Colour of Justice: Based on the Transcripts of the Stephen Lawrence Inquiry*. London: Oberon, 1999.

Pinter, Harold. 'Art, Truth and Politics.' Nobel Prize in Literature lecture, 7 Dec. 2005. 7 Dec. 2007 <http://nobelprize.org/nobel_prizes/literature/laureates/2005/pinter-lecture-e.html>.

Prentki, Tim, and Sheila Preston, eds. *The Applied Theatre Reader*. Abingdon, UK, and New York: Routledge, 2008.

Raad, Walid. *My Neck Is Thinner Than a Hair V. 2*. Manchester: Cornerhouse, 2006.

—————. *The Atlas Group (1989–2004)*. Cologne: Walther König, 2007.

Read, Alan *Theatre, Intimacy & Engagement. The Last Human Venue*. Houndmills, UK: Palgrave Macmillan, 2007.

Schechner, Richard, ed. *War and Other Bad Shit*. Spec. iss. of *The Drama Review* 52.1 (2008).

Shakespeare, William. *King Lear*. London: Penguin, 1972.

Taylor, Diana. *Disappearing Acts: Spectacles of Gender and Nationalism in Argentina's Dirty War*. Durham, NC: Duke UP, 1997.

—————. *The Archive and the Repertoire: Performing Cultural Memory in the Americas*. Durham, NC: Duke UP, 2003.

Taylor, Diana, and Sarah J. Townsend, eds. *Stages of Conflict: A Critical Anthology of Latin American Theater and Performance*. Trans. Margaret Carson. Ann Arbor: U of Michigan P, 2008.

Taylor, Jane, with William Kentridge and Handspring Puppet Company. 'Ubu and the Truth Commission.' 1997. *Postcolonial Plays: An Anthology*. Ed. Helen Gilbert. London and New York: Routledge, 2001. 29–47.

Thompson, James. *Applied Theatre: Bewilderment and Beyond*. Oxford and New York: Peter Lang, 2003.

—————. *Digging Up Stories: Applied Theatre, Performance and War*. Manchester: Manchester UP, 2006.

Thompson, James, and Richard Schechner, eds. *Social Theatre*. Spec. iss. of *The Drama Review* 48.3 (2004).

Van Erven, Eugène. *The Playful Revolution: Theatre and Liberation in Asia*. Bloomington and Indianapolis: Indiana UP, 1992.

Van Erven, Eugène. *Community Theatre: Global Perspectives*. London and New York: Routledge, 2000.

Winston, Joe, ed. *Citizenship, Human Rights and Applied Drama*. Spec. iss. of *Research in Drama Education* 12.3 (2007).

Websites of artists and projects discussed

Amrita Performing Arts: http://amritaperformingarts.org/
Ariel Dorfman: www.adorfman.duke.edu/
The Atlas Group: www.theatlasgroup.org/
Coco Fusco: www.cocofusco.com/
Drama Box: www.dramabox.org/english/index.html
The Exonerated: www.theexonerated.com/
Free Belarus Theatre: http://dramaturg.org/?lang=en
Handspring Puppet Company: www.handspringpuppet.co.za/
In Place of War: www.inplaceofwar.net/
Leibniz Performance Collective: www.leibnizlab.co.uk/
Ngapartji Ngapartji: www.ngapartji.org/
Speak Truth to Power: www.speaktruth.org/
Theatre of the Oppressed: www.theatreoftheoppressed.org/
TheatreWorks: www.theatreworks.org.sg/
Tricycle Theatre: www.tricycle.co.uk/
The Truth in Translation Project: www.truthintranslation.org/
V Day: www.vday.org/

Websites of human rights resources and NGOs

Amnesty International: www.amnesty.org/
Article 19: www.article19.org/
Freedom House: www.freedomhouse.org/
Human Rights Watch: www.hrw.org/
Index on Censorship: www.indexoncensorship.org/
International Criminal Court: www.icc-cpi.int/
International PEN: www.internationalpen.org.uk/
Liberty: www.liberty-human-rights.org.uk/
Open Democracy: www.opendemocracy.net/
Oxford Amnesty Lectures: www.oxford-amnesty-lectures.org/
New Tactics in Human Rights: www.newtactics.org/
UN Human Rights Homepage: www.un.org/rights/
UNESCO Culture Homepage: www.unesco.org/culture/
University of Minnesota Human Rights Library: www1.umn.edu/humanrts/
Witness: www.witness.org/

index